76

WAR ON THE LINE

The Story of the Southern Railway in War-Time

By

BERNARD DARWIN

FOREWORD

All who read this book will agree that the Southern Railway has been fortunate in obtaining the services of Mr. Bernard Darwin to tell the epic story of what Southern Railway men and women did in the war just ended. The contribution to victory made by Sir Eustace Missenden, the General Manager, and all his staff from top to bottom, will go down to history as a great achievement. And this book will, I hope, serve to remind not only the present generation, but those who come after, what devotion to duty and good team work in a great organisation really mean.

ERIC GORE BROWNE,
Chairman,
Southern Railway.

CHAIRMAN'S ROOM,
WATERLOO STATION,
LONDON, 1946.

PREFACE TO THE REPRINT

The Southern Railway achieved remarkable transport feats after Dunkirk and suffered dreadfully in the Blitz, but its greatest wartime undertaking was the movement of supplies for the Normandy landings. The 40th anniversary of D-Day is therefore an appropriate time to reprint this volume "for those who come after", as the Chairman wrote in 1946. Permission to do this has been kindly given by Mr. Richard Day, Regional Publicity Officer, British Rail (Southern).

First Published 1946
First reprint 1984
Second reprint 1993
Third reprint 1998

ISBN 0 906520 10 X

Reissued in 1984 by
Middleton Press
Easebourne Lane
Midhurst, West Sussex
GU29 9AZ
Tel: 01730 813169
Fax: 01730 812601

Reprinted & bound by Biddles Ltd,
Guildford and Kings Lynn

CONTENTS

Statistical information will be found at the end of various chapters and on pages 204 to 210.

ILLUSTRATIONS

COVER PHOTO

A Greyhound Class locomotive after a direct hit on Fratton Engine Shed.

Chapter 1

INTRODUCTORY

THIS attempt to tell the story of the Southern Railway in war-time was begun during the war, but a considerable part of it was written after peace had come. One small personal incident connected with it I can never forget as long as I live. I was driven down to see Southampton Docks on V.E. Day through a beflagged and rejoicing England, and one of the first things I saw there was a great ship crowded with American soldiers about to set out on their way home. But to say that the book was begun in war-time is much less than all the truth, though true as far as I myself am concerned. The records, without which I should have been helpless, had been systematically collected almost since the day on which war broke out, and indeed many of them go further back than that and refer to preparations made beforehand against that war's imminent and inevitable coming. The subject is so big, that in the end I seem scarcely to have done more than scratch the surface of it, but at least I have had no lack of material in which to delve deeper nor of kind helpers to light the path

This mass of records, sometimes almost appalling in its magnitude, has been compiled by railwaymen and the resulting summary, for I cannot hope to make it more, is the work of one who set out with a blank and virgin mind, completely innocent of railway knowledge. There are obvious dangers in such ignorance and one of them, which I have had constantly to bear in mind, is that the writer may be so fascinated by seeing this great complex machine for the first time from within, that he may forget that he is not trying to describe how the wheels go round but how they kept going round in war-time. Perhaps however there is some compensating advantage in his coming to it with a fresh mind. Being a complete amateur, a mere man in the street, he knows by instinct what will appeal to his brethren of the street and can appreciate things which are really very wonderful, but to the professional may appear merely part of the day's work. He may and doubtless does lack a sense of proportion, being struck with astonishment by facts which are by comparison simple and failing to grasp the intricacy of problems which are extremely difficult. But—and this is I think a real advantage—since he does not belong to the railway he is not oppressed with any false modesty about it and can openly give praise to things which are intensely deserving of it.

Many of these, if he had so much as heard of them, he would before have taken for granted. When he sees them a little nearer admiration and astonishment come over him in sudden gusts of understanding. For instance I have said elsewhere in this book something of the great Marshalling Yard at Feltham, which is, to use a name once very familiar during the war, the Hamm of the south of England. As I watched that apparent marvel of the sorting out of hundreds of wagons going on like clockwork on a fine sunny day of peace, it was suddenly borne in on me what that work must have been like on a bitter winter's night during an air raid. That moment of revelation, even if of most imperfect revelation, was, I hope, of value to me ever afterwards. Whatever I was shown I could do a kind of rule of three sum in my head; as peace-time is to war-time and as summer is to winter, so what I am seeing now is to the answer I want to get, the answer of what had to be done.

Much of this admiration which the outsider, such as I am, comes to feel for the railway must be derived from information which he gets second-hand, but there are one or two respects in which his own first-hand knowledge rams it home. He has had at least some experience of the " blitz." He knows how unpleasant it was even if he was in a shelter and how very much more unpleasant if he had to be abroad and carrying on. That enables him to do the rule of three sum I suggested. He knows too that, no matter what happened, the railway carried him to and from his daily work with wonderful regularity and, all things considered, with wonderfully little dis-comfort. This feat he has always to some extent appreciated, but he comes to appraise it much more at its proper worth when he dimly realises all the other people and all the other loads that the railway had to carry and in all the other trains. When he sees some of the statistics of troop trains and evacuation trains, of Dunkirk and of D-Day and the stores that had to be accumulated for that vast enter-prise, he begins to see that the carrying of his own insignificant self and of hundreds of thousands like him was an achievement indeed.

All the railways did great and strenuous work during the war. They became a closely knitted alliance to take their share, of infinite importance and having infinitely numerous ramifications, in the united effort of the war. But they did not lose their own entities and characters and each from its place on the map had its own particular part to play. It is not a boast but merely a statement of geographical fact that the Southern was predestined to play the greatest and most arduous part of all. It served that part of England which must be in most imminent danger of invasion if invasion came, and which must inevitably be the first and most constant target for air attack. It possessed in its own docks at Southampton the port which has long been synonymous with the departure of troops for foreign service and with the arrival of ships, and so in war-time of troops, from America. Its share in the war's work was not only the most intense and severe, but it was also the most dramatic. It moved the first British Expeditionary Force. Its name must be for ever connected with the great and complex movement which is known by the name of Dunkirk. Four years later it carried the invading armies on the last stage of their converging journeys, and Southampton was the very heart and nucleus of that still greater and long continued movement called D-Day, in which the 6th of June was only one single culminating event.

It is the legitimate boast of the country's railways that they were ready for the emergency. It may be that not till the hope of peace was almost gone did they make many specific preparations for war, but ever since the last war they had in a more general sense been making themselves ready. In swifter trains, in better rolling stock, in the devising of new locomotives and new vehicles for both

3

passengers and freight, in the renewing, enlarging and maintenance of tracks—in these and many other lesser ways they had steadily been increasing their fitness for the supreme ordeal. The Southern Railway had been getting ready in one particular direction, electrification. In the course of a five-year plan it has electrified in all 1,760 track miles. In peace-time this had enabled it to carry more passengers at a much greater speed and with a greater punctuality than before. In war-time it made it possible, despite all other and most urgent claims, to carry its regular passengers from their dormitory towns and villages to their daily work in an uninterrupted flow. In peace-time it had been pre-eminently a passenger line and the greatest passenger line. There were hardly any great industrial towns on its system; 75 per cent. of its traffic was a passenger traffic. In the handling of passengers it had had great and valuable practice. It was expert in moving crowds especially on the occasions of popular sporting events. It could move train loads of football spectators to Twickenham in such rapid succession that a second load had arrived before the first was off the platform. This experience was of immense value in the moving of great numbers of troops and of the workers in the new factories who had everywhere to be provided for. The war-time freight traffic increased in volume till it was a case of fifty-fifty with the greatly increased passenger traffic, but never for a moment did the line snap under the double strain.

In going to see various places on the Southern Railway and meeting some of those who do its work I have come, very humbly, to have an immense admiration for the railwayman and have been trying to analyse my feelings and see if I can say why. His spirit seems to me simply that of the English people at its best, that spirit which has so often been a baffling and irritating puzzle to other nations, which has pulled this country through its almost desperate ordeal of the last six years. The railwayman, as I see him, is entirely resolved not to be fussed or rattled and takes everything that happens as part of the day's work. I have never met a greater master of understatement. The Foreman Porter who told me that after a long drawn out strain of most dangerous work was over he " felt blooming queer " may stand for all his brethren. He will admit that some problem, whether sudden or continuous, was in the nature of a " headache," but that is as far as he is inclined to go and even that

4

admission must be extracted from him. It was certainly a bad night in the " blitz " on which perhaps only hand signalling was possible, but there it was and they got through with it. To his account of anything that befell him he gives a humorous twist. The joke may be now and then a little grim, but it is always there ; his sense of humour is perennial. Lastly he has a dogged determination not to be beaten, productive of almost endless sticking power and a fine three o'clock-in-the-morning courage.

I will not embarrass him by saying too much of this courage of his, but will rather emulate his gift of meiosis. Anybody who reads the chapter in this book on " Enemy Action " will, I hope, realise something at any rate of what he had to bear and how he went through with it. A small thought came into my head one day on this point and I set it down for what it is worth. I was at Deepdene, near Dorking, where were the Southern Railway's war-time headquarters, and happened to see some of the team of despatch riders about to set out on their motor bicycles. Deepdene is a green and pleasant and peaceful spot, that was untroubled by bombs and must have seemed in the worst times of the blitz a restful haven.* But every night during the raids some of those despatch riders would leave the quiet of Deepdene to plunge into London on their missions, seeing fires perhaps coming ever nearer to them, and no single one of them during all the war years ever hesitated to go or having gone ever turned back. The contrast struck me so forcibly that I have here recorded the impression, and yet is no more than one example, and those despatch riders had not had more to brave than thousands of other railwaymen, or for that matter I daresay thousands of others in all walks of life. But because courage was common it was not the less great on that account, nor is it the less worthy of eulogy.

Another point that has struck me, and that I venture to name, is the feeling of loyalty and friendliness and comradeship which railwaymen have towards the railway and one another. I must add railwaywomen, since everywhere I have been told how splendidly the women worked, and in a number of places, notably at Redbridge where they outnumber the men, I have seen them with my own admiring eyes. Indeed the word " railwayman " must now be taken to include both sexes. The expression " team spirit " is a rather tiresome one and is sometimes perhaps worked too hard, but I admit

* There were several fatalities in Dorking due to bombing.

I cannot think of a better for my purpose. The railwayman seems to have it in generous measure. The Southern Railway represents a fusion and not yet a very old one of the South Eastern, the London Brighton and the South Western, but of all those that I have met I know as to hardly one of them to which he originally belonged, so well united is the team to-day. And this spirit has, I am sure, been of incalculable value during the war years, not merely in the every-day work but in the additional duties, such as those of fire fighters, spotters, the Home Guard and the rest, to which the railwaymen gave so ungrudgingly of their scanty leisure. This spirit is a very real and living thing and is, as I should judge, greatly enhanced by the often hereditary nature of the railwayman's occupation. To the stranger it is both pleasant and surprising to find how common and how strong is this hereditary link, and what a number of railway families there are in which the son, and now the daughter too, follows the father almost as a matter of course in the family calling. There is something both engaging and moving in the knowledge that the youngest woman guard, let us say, has a father who was a guard before her and a brother who is a porter, and a sister who has married into the railway, and so on through the ramifications of several families. This must surely produce a fine sense of brotherhood, an " old school tie " feeling in the best sense of those often abused words, a genuine bond between those who have gone before and those who will come after, of immeasurable value in times of stress.

In saying these few things I feel, as I said before, very humble, lest they should imply on the one hand condescension—and heaven knows I am there guiltless—and on the other the assumption of a knowledge I do not possess. There is one more as to which I hesitate still further, and yet I will be brave and say in so many words that the Southern Railway has impressed at least one ignorant outsider as an enterprise of extreme efficiency. It would be an impertinence for me to praise Sir Eustace Missenden, the General Manager, who has seen the war through from begining to end, but I may thank him for much kindly encouragement and for giving me a free hand. What may be the railways' future in these days of the melting pot, no one, I suppose, can tell, but I find it hard to believe that under any other regime it can be conducted with greater keenness and success or with a finer or more loyal tradition. I will only add Floreat, Florebit !

Chapter I

DUNKIRK

Part I

EARLY in May, 1940, the position of the Allied forces was gravely compromised. " They may not be able to hold the Channel Ports " ; how well I remember—and everyone must have some such memories—the shock of hearing those words spoken by one who had every chance of knowing what was what. Very soon that doubt had become a certainty. On the 13th of May military traffic was still going outwards by the Dunkirk Ferry, but the Germans were now sweeping in a flood across Northern France, and by the 17th all the ports of North East France were closed. Three days later the service between Havre and Southampton was cancelled. Three days later again, on the 23rd, the Boulogne Harbour officials and workmen were evacuated and reached England in any and every type of vessel. On the evening of the 27th the ominous code word " Dynamo," which stood for the scheme for evacuating the British Army, was given, and the fateful nine days which will for ever be known by the comprehensive name of Dunkirk began.

In this scheme the Southern Railway's main role was that of carrying the troops by train when they had landed in England, but the Railway can claim another and a highly honourable share in it through their ships. It was the Admiralty's part to collect the gallant and heterogeneous fleet which seemed almost miraculously to spring into being at the call, the pleasure steamers, coasting vessels, Thames steamers, motor barges, tugs and every conceivable kind of

7

small craft to whom so much was and is due. All told 220 Allied
Naval vessels and 650 other vessels were engaged, but the cross-
channel boats of the Southern Railway, many of their names once so
familiar to holiday-makers, now turned to sterner tasks, have one and
all a great record on their own account in this evacuation, which if
not a victory was yet a triumph, and it is of them that I propose to say
something here.

A number of them had from the beginning of the war been
chartered by the Admiralty either as military transports or hospital
carriers. Here are their names and it is to be hoped that those that
have survived will be marked when they return to their peaceful
avocations, by some modest plaque which need bear but the single
word " Dunkirk." Hospital Carriers : *Maid of Kent, Brighton, Isle of
Thanet, Isle of Guernsey, Dinard, Paris, Worthing.* Military Transports :
*Normannia, Lorina, Biarritz, Canterbury, Maid of Orleans, Whitstable,
Autocarrier, Hythe.* These names, however, by no means complete
the list. On May the 29th the *Brittany* was taken over by the Government and warning given that *St. Briac* and *Isle of Sark* might be wanted.
At noon on the same day a signal was received, " All available Southern
Railway steamers of 1,000 tons gross with a range of 150 miles are
required for immediate Government service." The cargo boats
Whitstable and *Hythe* were instantly handed over ; *Deal* was held in
readiness and ultimately there were also requisitioned *St. Briac,
Whippingham, Portsdown, Fishbourne, Wootton* and *Foremost II.* " There
be of them that have left a name behind them."

Five were lost, two of them before the " Dynamo " move began.
On May 23rd the *Maid of Kent*, while loaded with wounded, was
hit by five bombs and sank in the harbour at Dieppe ; the *Brighton*
was likewise bombed and sunk. Both were clearly marked as hospital
ships and the attacks must have been as perfectly deliberate as were
those on other hospital ships that succeeded them.

On the 30th the transports *Lorina* and *Normannia* were sunk
at Dunkirk, though all the *Normannia's* crew reached England in
safety. Their sister ships on their voyages to and from Dunkirk
saw them as they passed by, the *Lorina* aground with her back
broken, the *Normannia* with her funnels and masts showing above
the water, and her flag still bravely flying. Admiral Duncan would

8

have liked that. It is recorded of him how lying off the Texel
in 1797 with his own flagship and one other vessel, he heard that the
whole of the Dutch fleet was putting to sea. He anchored his two
ships and prepared to fight, saying " I have taken the depth of the
water, and when the *Venerable* goes down her flag will still fly."
On June 2nd the *Paris*, another hospital ship, was attacked by
bombs and so severely damaged that she had to be abandoned and
ultimately sank.

I must try to give some account of the adventures of these ships,
though how to do it is a problem. To take them one by one, even
though they all deserve it, would make too long drawn out a story,
and the best plan seems to be to take the days one by one and make a
composite diary for the Southern Railway ships. There is bound to
be a certain monotony because the incidents were in a large measure
the same, but a monotony of constant danger, faced with constant
valour is, I hope, one at least partially to disarm the most impatient.
Before beginning this attempt at a diary there are one or two general
things to say.

First: the danger near the French coast was as near as might
be continuous, even though a handful of our fighter planes showed
that mastery of their opponents, which later was to be so nobly
exhibited in the Battle of Britain. A single sentence from a report of
one of his trips by Captain Walker of the *Maid of Orleans* is eloquent.
" Subjected as usual to attacks from bombing planes." That
says a great deal, but it does not say all, for the ships were also
shelled more or less regularly from Gravelines, from Calais, from
nearer Dunkirk itself. The conditions did indeed vary. Sometimes a
thick pall of smoke hung over Dunkirk, making a ship a less visible
mark for a bomb. Sometimes the quays were brilliantly lighted up by
surrounding fires, in which the glistening white of the hospital ships
was an all too clear inducement to the enemy airmen who attacked
them with cold deliberation. At first, embarkation took place
throughout the twenty-four hours, but as the situation became more
and more difficult this was only possible at night; but whether by
night or day there was always danger.

Second: the larger vessels, and in particular of course the
hospital ships, had to be moored at pier or jetty, and, apart from the

9

question of room, it became increasingly hard as the days wore on because these had been damaged by shells and bombs. The smaller craft had a different technique, dealing direct with the beaches, and I pass on this account of it from the Master of the *Whitstable* : " The method used for embarking the troops from the beach was that the soldiers rowed off in boats until they were in water deep enough for shallow draft launches to take them in tow. The launches then towed the boats to the ships at anchor, who in turn carried the troops to a home port."

Third : since only the voyages of a few ships can be touched on the reader may, even though he knows better, find himself imagining them in an empty sea. He must constantly remember, as I try to do, that the sea was full of craft of every kind, that they were travelling without lights sometimes in misty weather, and it was through them, to say nothing of wrecks and minefields, that a way must be threaded.

Fourth : there was little enough time between a ship arriving at Dover, or some other port, before she set out for Dunkirk again, but such time as there was was not one of rest and surcease. There was often the dreadful task of sorting the living from the dead. Further, most of the men's equipment was left on the ship and all this had to be cleared before she could start again. There was also the difficult question of oil and coal. There was a large supply of coal on the spot, but some more was brought in special trains from Betteshanger Colliery.

With that introduction I will start with the 25th of May, two days before the evacuation technically began, but when the conditions were essentially " Dynamo " conditions. First shall come the *Canterbury* (Captain Hancock), " one of the pomps of yesterday," as the boat that carried the passengers travelling in state and luxury by the *Golden Arrow* train. When I was at Southampton Docks I chanced to see her, scarcely looking her old part in her grim grey coat, but doubtless as Captain Flint said of his *Walrus*, " She'll beat up for more, by thunder ! "

At a little before three o'clock on the afternoon of the 25th, not long returned from another crossing, the *Canterbury* set out for Dunkirk. She was shelled by German batteries on the way, embarked

1,246 men and left at 6.50, was at Dover by half past nine, anchored at midnight and remained under immediate steam against her next voyage. Later on the same day the two hospital ships, *Isle of Thanet* (Captain Hammond) and *Paris* (Captain Biles), were ordered to Dunkirk. Ships off Calais between them and the shore were being shelled by batteries in a wood west of Calais. At Dunkirk they moored alongside the *Canterbury*, and when she had sailed the *Isle of Thanet* took the quayside and began loading at ten o'clock. There were fires in the Docks lighting up the quayside, and constant air attacks. The *Isle of Thanet* was sprayed with shrapnel and one salvo of bombs fell very close. The loading in these conditions took nearly three hours, but at last 608 casualties were on board and she sailed for Newhaven, the *Paris* following, and both reaching port unscathed on the morning of the 26th.

On that same morning of the 26th the *Maid of Orleans* (Captain Walker) started for Dunkirk carrying water and various stores, and a detachment of 250 troops. She reached Dunkirk through shelling, but could not enter and returned to Dover. There she received orders to set out again, this time with an escort, and arrived safely about half past five. She landed her men and stores and discharged her water by forming a chain from well deck to gangway. A thick pall of smoke from burning oil reservoirs hid the ship. She took just under a thousand men on board and left at three in the morning. Meanwhile the *Canterbury* had appeared again and berthed outside the *Maid of Orleans*. She arrived at 8.30 and loaded 1,340 men under almost continuous bombing, and was away again soon after midnight. Earlier in the day two more hospital ships had come into this composite picture, the *Isle of Guernsey* (Captain Hodges) and the *Worthing* (Captain Munton). They sailed with a transport, the *Mona's Queen*, and as they drew near Calais, lying in ruins under a cloud of smoke, a little battle developed. Two British destroyers crossed their bows and began to shell the shore batteries, which instantly responded. This involved a deviation from a course which would have taken them between the combatants, and while they were changing their course enemy planes appeared and attacked them. The bombs fell very close but missed, and they reached Dunkirk to find a stream of motor ambulances threading their way between the less severely wounded who could still walk. Both the hospital ships were soon loaded as full as was humanly possible ; the *Isle of Guernsey* having only cots for 203 carried 346 men, many having to lie between the cots, on deck, in the corridors or anywhere where it was possible to insinuate a stretcher. They reached Newhaven safely, unloaded, took in oil fuel, water, and provisions, and then back again to Dover for orders.

Now to the 27th, which was a hard and bad day. The *Canterbury* after five and a half hours' interval was off again, reached Dunkirk at 8.0 p.m., loaded 457 troops, most of them wounded and including 140 stretcher cases, in 58 minutes, and started home again. The conditions were bad, and the bombing so continuous that the *Canterbury* had orders to turn back any vessel trying to reach Dunkirk that night, and she did turn back accordingly the *Maid of Orleans* (she had only reached Dover at six o'clock that evening and was setting out yet again), and two hospital ships ; one of these, the *Isle of Thanet*, had a collision on the way home, which put a temporary stop to her career. The return journey was the less pleasant from the constant dropping of parachute flares by enemy aircraft. The most trying experience of this day was, however, that of the *Biarritz* (Captain Baker). She was passing Gravelines on her way to Dunkirk when an enemy battery on shore attacked her, and the first shell entered the forward boiler room and severely wounded a very brave man, Fireman Phillips, who died that night. Though badly hit in the thigh he tried hard to close the oil fuel supply to the furnace of the two forward boilers. He failed, but had still strength to climb two flights of ladders out of the boiler room, and report to the Captain before he collapsed. Mr. Crockart, the Engineer in charge, who was subsequently decorated for his courageous conduct, succeeded in closing the supply of fuel to the forward boilers, but it was impossible to locate the damage in the forward boiler room and way must be kept on the ship, both in order to get out of range and not to stop in the minefield into which the ship had to be turned. The *Biarritz* got bravely home, and I have since seen her discharging a cheerful leave party at Dover, but she naturally could take no further part in the epic of Dunkirk.

The 28th seems to have been for most of the Southern Ships a day that might almost be called one of rest, but it was not so for the Hospital ship *Dinard* (Captain Allwyn Jones) on the first of her two trips to Dunkirk. She berthed alongside the pier and the crew and the R.A.M.C. staff had a very hard time of it getting the wounded men on board. There were no gang planks supplied, so that any form of improvised plank had to be used that would span the space between the pier and the ship, which obstinately refused to stay still alongside; 271 stretcher cases were got on board, but that was far from ending the adventures of the night. The Channel was hard to find since several of the light buoys were not functioning; the night was misty and the sea alive with craft showing no light. One destroyer going very fast actually touched the ship's belting, and as a culmination two torpedoes were discharged at the *Dinard*. "The water being very luminous that night" remarks the Master cheerily "it was very easy to see and avoid the attack." I must take the gallant officer's word for it, but it does not sound so very easy.

On the 30th our now old friends the *Maid of Orleans* and the *Canterbury* are at it again. The *Maid of Orleans* had to spend five hours alongside the pier which was being shelled, embarked 1,372 troops and was bombed on her way back to Dover. Incidentally she stopped off Nieuport and picked up two French officers who were trying to reach England in a small open boat. The *Canterbury* had in point of hours a rather less trying time, for she was at Dunkirk ten minutes under the three hours before leaving with 1,950 troops. In that time, however, she had had several dive-bombing attacks, and on the way home one salvo fell so near that she was damaged and must have a little compulsory rest for repairs in the Granville Dock. The *Isle of Guernsey* hospital ship had also on this day a voyage decidedly eventful. Except for torpedoes she seems to have had a little of everything. Of all the terse, vivid and modest descriptions written by the various Masters, I think that, were I an examiner for a prize essay, I should give the prize to the Master of the *Isle of Guernsey*, and so I take leave to set it out in full:—

" May 29th, 1940 : At 5.16 p.m. having received orders, we proceeded towards Dunkirk following a course which took us well clear of Calais. At 7.12 p.m. we stood off for a while because of an engagement between aircraft and a British destroyer immediately in our track. At 7.30 p.m. an airman was observed descending by parachute close ahead of us and the vessel was stopped to save him. One of the seamen went down a rope ladder to assist the airman, but before he reached the bottom, ten enemy planes attacked the ship with bombs, cannon and machine gun. By a miracle none of the bombs struck the ship, although considerable damage was done by the concussion, shrapnel, cannon shells and machine gun bullets. British fighter planes drove off the enemy, and we proceeded towards Dunkirk with a terrific air battle taking place overhead. Arrived off the port at 8.20 p.m. we found it being bombed and shelled, and we had orders from the shore to keep clear. Returning along the Channel in company with two destroyers we later received orders to wait until darkness had fallen, and then return to Dunkirk. At 11.30 p.m. we entered between the fires, burning oil tanks, etc., and managed to moor up alongside what was left of the quay at 12.30 a.m. Loading commenced at once, by 2.15 a.m. we had taken on board as many as we could, numbering 490. All the crew and R.A.M.C. personnel behaved splendidly throughout, carrying on with their duties and doing their utmost to load the ship as quickly and as fully as possible, although the ship was shaken every few minutes by the explosion of bombs falling on the quay and in the water. Leaving the quay at 2.15 a.m. we proceeded out of the harbour and just outside we found the sea full of men swimming and shouting for help ; presumably a transport had just been sunk. As two destroyers were standing by picking these men up, we threaded our way carefully through them and proceeded towards Dover. It would have been fatal for us to attempt to stop and try to save any of these men, as we made such a wonderful target for the aircraft hovering overhead, with the flames of the port showing all our white paintwork up. Everything was comparatively quiet on the way across, except that just before we got to Dover a patrol boat headed us off as we were heading straight for a recently laid minefield. Arriving off Dover at 7.0 a.m. we received orders to proceed to Newhaven and arrived at that port at 11.15 a.m."

After those crowded eighteen hours—and I find myself giving a sigh of thankfulness when the ship is safe home—the *Isle of Guernsey* had to retire for her wounds to be healed, and by the time she was fit to sail again the evacuation was over.

On the 30th the *Dinard* had her second trip to Dunkirk accompanied by constant shelling and bombing, and Verey lights to give the range overhead. Again there was the greatest difficulty with improvised gangways to a ship that was constantly rocking from the enemy's " near misses." At last when the shells were regularly bursting within twenty yards and the water had fallen so that the ship was barely afloat, the *Dinard* backed out, made her way with an electric torch to identify the buoys, remained under shell fire until the end of the channel, and so home. The *Maid of Orleans* was there again too, " bombed as usual," with only one berth now usable since the pier had been badly damaged by shells and bombs. Still she embarked over 1,250 men; many of them were wounded, and forty-two were stretcher cases that had to be made as comfortable as might be in what had once been the Restaurant and the Saloon.

Another ship figures for the first time in to-day's story. When the cargo boat *Hythe* (Captain Morford), just taken over by the Government, had her first jaunt to Dunkirk, the Captain's instructions were to patrol No. 3 Beach and pick up as many troops as he could. He was welcomed by bombs from an enemy squadron which was attacked by our fighters, reached his appointed beach and waited for boats ; but the surf was such that the boats could not leave the beach. Thereupon he decided on his own initiative to enter Dunkirk, and, greeted by a salvo of shells, berthed at a jetty. After five hours of more or less incessant attack he had collected over 650 men. There was room, he regretfully says, for perhaps twenty more, but the shelling was so heavy that the Naval Embarkation Officer ordered him away and he returned " uneventfully " to Dover.

On the next day, May 31st, it was the turn of the *Whitstable* (Captain Baxter), which had been requisitioned with the *Hythe*. Her orders were to go to a position five miles east of Dunkirk and pick up troops. She had a weary, gruelling time of waiting, with air battles overhead and shells drawing unattractively near, and though she anchored at a place called Bray at 8.20 a.m. she did not leave her anchorage till seven hours later. During all that time only one boat with troops came alongside and her disappointing haul was just fourteen men.

The 1st of June saw the *Maid of Orleans* at Dunkirk yet again. She arrived just before daybreak, but had to stay there six hours while two destroyers loaded troops over her decks, since the *Maid's* gangways were the more efficient. When the destroyers had loaded she herself took on board 1,856 men, including 400 French troops, and then made her way home in broad daylight with bombers persistently attentive. On the same evening she was ordered back yet again, but this was not to be, for while leaving Dover Harbour she collided with H.M.S. *Worcester* and the need for repairs brought her fine career to an end. In all she had carried from Dunkirk 5,469 men, and her Master, Captain Walker, received the D.S.C.

The number of the Southern ships available had now grown considerably smaller, and on the 2nd it was reduced by the loss of the hospital ship *Paris*. The other hospital ship, the *Worthing*, started first on that day just before 1.0 p.m., and within an hour was attacked by an enemy bomber which first dived and machine-gunned the ship and then dropped nine heavy bombs—as sustained and calculated an attack on a hospital ship as can be imagined. The ship was swinging very fast on her helm and the bombs missed her, but some fell within three or four feet doing serious damage, and she must turn for home. The *Paris* sailing some two hours later intercepted a wireless message saying that the *Worthing* was being heavily bombed, and the Captain thereupon asked for orders. Two hours later he was told to proceed. Soon afterwards the ship was attacked by two enemy aircraft and their bombs fell so close that steam pipes burst in the engine room, the ship was out of all control and the Captain ordered the life boats to be swung out to boat deck

These little ships came from France in their hundreds, seeking refuge in
Southampton

The gateway from the Continent. French survivors from Dunkirk arrive
at Dover Marine Station

Today Saturday June 1st
The Reigate portions of all trains are cancelled
The Train service between Redhill & Tonbridge & Redhill
& Reading are cancelled.
Buses will be provided between Redhill & Tonbridge
. Redhill & Guildford. .

All trains booked to call at Redhill will call at Earlswood
Bus from Earlswood to Redhill.
Passengers for Coulsdon South & Merstham travel by usual Trains
& change at Coulsdon North thence by Bus.

Civilian passenger trains were entirely suspended on important cross-country
lines to free the lines for Dunkirk specials

Voluntary workers organised the feeding of the troops from Dunkirk at
Headcorn, Tonbridge and elsewhere

A German bomb landed on the main line south of Horsham in 1940 and a goods train ran into the crater

level, and part of the crew to take their stations in them. The ship was found not to be making water; so he decided to keep the rest of the crew on board in the hope of a rescue ship from Dover. He then hoisted distress signals and fired rockets which produced three more enemy planes, and as the result of a bomb all the men in one life boat were thrown into the water. The other life boats were then lowered and sent to the rescue, and only the Master, the Chief Officer and the Quarter Master were left on board. At this crisis a speed boat appeared, took them off, picked up all the life boats and towed them until relieved by a tug. From the first attack till the arrival of the speed boat there was no ship in sight save one mysterious and sinister motor craft believed by the Captain to be a decoy, which paid no attention to any signal of distress, but on the ship being bombed again raced away. The *Paris* was abandoned and later sank. In all these stories many brave people must go unnamed, but an exception may be made for Mrs. Lee, a carriage cleaner at Brighton, who was a stewardess on the *Paris* on all her voyages to and from Dunkirk. She was thrown into the water and machine-gunned there; picked up by a life boat and blown out of it again, a hundred yards into the water. There she spent an hour and a half before being once more picked up and taken by the tug into Dover.

The last trip of the *Paris* coincided with the first of the *Autocarrier* (Captain Masters), which in peace-time had provided the motor car service from Dover to Calais. On her first voyage she was unlucky enough to draw blank, for there was not a soul to be seen on the jetty at Dunkirk, and after waiting nearly an hour amid much shelling there was nothing for it but to return to Dover. On June 3rd, however, she was more fortunate, and through continuous gun fire brought home 712 men. Meanwhile the *Canterbury*, repaired and once more eager for the fray, undocked and set out for Dunkirk, getting there a little before midnight. Under various difficulties she embarked something under 700 French troops, and then with the water falling and considerable risk of being grounded she had to leave Dunkirk for the last time. The 4th of June saw the end of the evacuation and the *Canterbury's* last voyage home was also the last for any of the Southern ships. It was one of these by the way that carried the greatest number of men on any single voyage. This was the *Whippingham*, a small paddle steamer, and her record was 2,700 men. These voyages have been very simply told with no attempt at heroics, but I hope something of their real heroism may shine through and illumine a prosaic narrative. Multiply the heroism of these few ships' crews by the number of all the other craft that played their part, and you have the sum total of endurance and courage which will for ever be freshly remembered at the name of Dunkirk.

THE SOUTHERN RAILWAY FLEET

September 3rd, 1939

Cross Channel Passenger Vessels (including Train Ferry and Motor Car Vessels	20
Cargo Vessels	9
Isle of Wight Vessels	13

S.R. Vessels lost through enemy action.

Cross Channel Passenger Vessels :

Lorina.	Paris.
Normannia.	Maid of Kent.
St. Briac.	Maid of Orleans.
Brighton.	

Cargo Vessels :

Minster.	Tonbridge.
Fratton.	

Isle of Wight Steamers :

Portsdown.	Southsea.

DUNKIRK

PART II

So much for the ships that brought the men so gallantly from France, and now for the second part of "the miracle of Dunkirk," only less miraculous than the first, the carrying of the men from the coast by train. How many of these there would be nobody knew, but Mr. Churchill told the House of Commons that not 335,000 but 20,000 or 30,000 had been expected. How many of them would land at any one port at any one time nobody knew either, and where they were going to when they had landed, the men who drove the engines very often did not know. Sometimes they thought they did, but the military authorities changed their mind about it while they were on their way. "Stop at Guildford and ask where you're going to" was a typical instruction given, as were all instructions, by word of mouth. And yet the whole process from the 27th of May till the 4th of June went like clockwork. Train after train drew up; each was filled with tired grimy men, "with a bun in one hand and a banana in the other," as Mr. Steward, the Marine Superintendent at Dover, described it to me, and, twenty minutes or so after its predecessor, rolled away into the blue, while another took its place. The railways knew that in the nature of things they could get but short notice, and short it was. "Dynamo," that not inappropriate code word for the scheme, was received at five o'clock in the afternoon of Sunday the 26th. By dawn on the 27th the procession of trains had begun.

Whatever the precise or even approximate number of men that might be coming one thing was clear—that an immense number of coaches would be wanted and wanted quickly. The Railway Companies in conference decided to form a pool of coaches. The

23

G.W.R. was to provide 40 trains, the L.M.S. 44, the L.N.E.R. 47 and the Southern 55—186 trains, in all involving nearly 2,000 vehicles. It was utterly uncertain at which ports the men might arrive, so the Southern Railway had to be ready to cover seven in all. Dover in fact had the lion's share with 327 trains, Folkestone had 64, Ramsgate 82, Margate 75 together with 21 ambulance trains, and Sheerness 17. In addition, some men were landed at Newhaven and some as far west as Southampton. Subject to fluctuations the rush was a steadily increasing one, and reached its climax on June 1st. Yet the 1st has a serious competitor in the 4th of June, when there were sixty vessels of one sort or another simultaneously alongside at Dover, and all those passengers must be cleared and packed into trains.

How was this truly remarkable task so triumphantly achieved ? The Southern Railway had been well accustomed to plan for big crowds and exceptional traffic in days of peace. There had been the Derby with 600 specials in a day to fit in among the normal trains ; there had been football matches at Twickenham or Charlton ; a Naval Review ; the Schneider Cup ; Ascot and so on. But in such cases there had been no element of the unexpected ; there had been time to plan in advance and past experience to go on. A highly detailed timetable with all its complexities of engine working, carriage working and special staff had always been produced beforehand. Dunkirk was different ; there was nothing to go on and a different method was needed. Improvisation and word of mouth were the order of the day, and if ever the telephone proved its worth it did so now. The Superintendent of Operations, Mr. Wheeler, instantly picked his best men and sent them to the scene of action with full powers. Priority for staff, for rolling stock and for telephones was given them and they did the rest. " If only " exclaimed a General " the Army could operate with as few written instructions as the Southern Railway does ! "

To the uninitiated it would seem that chaos was bound to ensue ; but all was smoothness and order, ensured, very briefly, by a system of controls at short intervals along the line. By way of example, as soon as the word " Dynamo " was received the Divisional Superintendent at Orpington held a meeting of his assistants, and sub-control offices were there and then set up at Dover Marine, Tonbridge,

Ashford, Faversham, Chatham and Dartford. Inspectors were placed at the two Dover and the two Folkestone Stations, at Ramsgate, Margate, Ashford, Headcorn, Paddock Wood and Faversham. On another part of the line there were sub-controls at Haywards Heath, Chichester and Shalford. There were two Liaison Officers appointed who were in constant touch with the military authorities at Dover Marine, one by day and the other by night. Empty trains were held at Queenborough, Faversham, Margate and Ramsgate, and the fear of not having enough of these empty trains and the problem of handling them, were two ever present anxieties, especially at Dover where the numbers of men were sometimes almost overwhelming. Yet in the end empty trains from other railway systems came so thick and fast that at one time four of them were held at Willesden since they could not be accepted at the ports.

These names and facts may give some notion of the problem, but it is a very faint one, for the trains were not all going, as the names might at first sight suggest, on the eastern part of the Southern line. Hundreds of them had to diverge to the west and travel over other systems. The French troops for instance had to get to Bournemouth and thence by Plymouth back to France. Yeovil, Tidworth Dorchester, Ludgershall, Bulford, Southampton, Blandford, Exeter, Salisbury, Plymouth, Devonport, Weymouth, Warminster—I copy them down as they occur, some of them again and again for page after page and column after column, and in the next column devoted to their route comes the single recurring name of Woking. But before they reached Woking they had to get to Redhill which was at the very heart of it all, the focus of this gigantic movement.

Redhill Junction is on the main line from London to Brighton, and from it diverge lines to Tonbridge, Dover, Guildford, Reading and Woking. It was, therefore, the obvious key point where should take place a great turning movement. Practically all the engines involved had to be coaled and watered there, and water once ran short despite every conceivable effort; it was nobody's fault, the supply simply could not cope with the demand. Labourers had to be imported from the country round. Some 300 tons of ashes accumulated at Redhill during the "Dynamo" time. Of all the loaded trains that ran from Dover to their various destinations in the south and west of England, more than 80 per cent. were dealt with at Redhill, and the utmost speed was essential. Many trains were cleared in four minutes ; the record holder was one which arrived at Redhill, changed engines and set off again in two minutes 30 seconds, and the layout of Redhill necessitated a rather complex process. This involved the providing of a second engine, technically known as a " turnover " at the rear of the train, and a turnover was wanted for every train going either from east to west or south to east or west and vice versa. Moreover, as the movements of loaded trains from east to west and empty trains from west to east constantly coincided the movement was practically continuous.

Then there were the engines to be dealt with when they were released from their trains by their turnovers. They were segregated on the Down line, ready to be despatched to the Loco Yard whenever there was a chance, and the chance did not always come when it was wanted. In the end the engines accumulated into trains on their own account, and would periodically be seen, in the words of Mr. Maitland from Nine Elms who had been put in charge at Redhill, " Cantering along towards the loco yard entrance at Earlswood." It would have been a sight to bring unique joy to the heart of a railway lover, but apparently it would not do, and later the engines were sent off in pairs. When the Yard could take no more the next pair would be sent off to Three Bridges to be coaled there, thus saving the honour of the gallant yard staff who would have died rather than admit that the job had beaten them.

There were other things that brought a moment's space to breathe, such as a stop for refreshments either at Headcorn or Paddock Wood, which was instituted after a day or two. That prevented the loaded trains from silting up quite so fast as they had done. An ambulance train demanding and given priority was also an occasional blessing. The empty trains on the other hand that were returning to the ports were, as Mr. Maitland says, " subject to no such moderating influence and had a nasty habit of appearing in blocks of a dozen or so unannounced." This problem of the empty trains moreover grew more troublesome towards the end of the move when evacuation from Dunkirk was possible only at night time.

Such, very briefly and imperfectly touched upon, were a few of the difficulties at Redhill, but the trains were not safe in any placid haven when Redhill was passed. Far from it, for there was another nightmare of turning to be undergone at Woking. Here as described for me is one of the little problems. " Another difficulty was that of turning engines at Woking, and many large engines had to run light via the Addlestone Triangle. This involved running from Woking to Weybridge, entering the bay platform on the Up side, running round the Spur line to Addlestone Junction and running back along the other Spur line on the Down Main line." No doubt many people with a better eye for railway country than I have can clearly visualise that operation. To me it is a little dark, but it sounds— it really does sound—complicated, and there was this additional difficulty that many of the drivers did not know the signals between Woking and Weybridge. In the case of men having to drive on lines strange to them, which naturally arose with drivers called from all over England, pilots were, if possible given, but the supply of pilots ran short and so Mr. Powell of Woking had often to tell the drivers orally about the signals at Weybridge so that they should deal with the curve at Addlestone.

These are just a few of the technical troubles described in untechnical language, enough I hope to give the reader some notion of these straining struggling days from the railwaymen's point of view. Morning, noon and night the strain went on, and rests were short and far between. Nobody thought of the long hours, but was ready to do one more turn of duty if it was wanted. And it is to be remembered that " Dynamo " was not all ; sandwiched in somehow between troop trains were others evacuating children from the coast. *The Times* had a leading article on the subject, commending the railways " especially the Southern Railway, which has conjured up at short notice a smooth and seemingly endless succession of trains, and has lavished upon the emergency its great and peculiar experience of the handling of masses." Olympian praise was never better deserved.

I have tried first as best I can to give some account of how the Railway staff grappled with its problem and brought their task to a happy issue with never a breakdown ; but there remains the story of more human and less mechanical achievement in which the Army and many devoted civilian helpers came in for their share of the Railway's glory. Those 330,000 men who arrived hungry, sleepy and exhausted from their long-drawn-out ordeal first on the Dunkirk beaches, and then on their crowded and perilous voyage, had all to be fed on their way to their diverse destinations, and that is a piece of catering at short notice to test, if not to appal, the most efficient. The Army was primarily responsible for it, and the R.A.S.C. did their job well and truly, but they were wonderfully reinforced by civilian helpers, and if the returning soldiers were not killed by kindness it was certainly not the fault of the dwellers by the lines over which they travelled. At only one place, as far as I can discover, was there even a threat of a breakdown in the feeding arrangements. That was at Basingstoke, where it seems that for a moment some question of red-tape and guaranteed payment woefully intervened. There may well be an amnesty in that direction now, and at any rate this possibility of official collapse was the civilians' great opportunity. The Mayor of Basingstoke and an energetic lady in the neighbourhood quickly mobilised a band of volunteers and raised and spent a sum of about £500, of which £100 was contributed by the staff at Thornycrofts' Works. There were a hundred lady helpers, the local A.F.S., the Fire Brigade, the Rotarians, the Church of England and the Free Churches, all blended in one harmonious whole. The bakers and confectioners worked day and night, and probably for the tired soldiers clouds of happy repletion now lie thick over the memories of Basingstoke.

That was of course at a later stage of the journey. Headcorn or Paddock Wood was the first stopping place for food, and Headcorn, till that time a station of comparatively modest celebrity, with a staff of a Station Master and two porters, leaped suddenly into fame (it was anonymous fame in those discreet times) by feeding 145,000 troops. The R.A.S.C. provided the food and forty soldiers to hand it out, but these forty were helped by forty to fifty ladies of the neighbourhood. For nine days and nights they worked in shifts of eight hours each; but eight hours were often not enough to satisfy their enthusiasm, and one of them stayed on duty continuously for twenty-four hours. Their headquarters was a large barn where the food was made ready and then carried across some fields, and across the line to the Up platform. One lady cut so many sandwiches that she declared she never wanted to eat a sandwich or anything else again. And yet sandwiches were but one choice in that stupendous bill of fare. For the mere sensual pleasure of writing them down let me record jellied veal, sardines, cheese, oranges and apples and that culminating romance of every railway lunch the hard boiled egg. Hard boiled eggs were reckoned in thousands ; so were meat pies and rolls and sausages. Five thousand of each of these last three delicacies appeared at Headcorn one evening, and by the next evening they " were not, translated unaware." Such noble viands were washed down by oceans of tea and coffee, in the making of which nineteen stoves were unresting night or day. The whole of Kent could hardly have produced cups enough and the drinks were handed into the trains in tin cans. When time was up the R.A.S.C. on the platform shouted to the B.E.F. in the train " Sling them out " ; a shower of tin clattered on to the platform, the train passed away and the staff, amateur and professional, at Headcorn fell to washing the cans and preparing for the next train. Many of the men in those trains had had very little sleep for days on end, and came into the station sunk in a deep slumber of exhaustion, but they never failed to wake up and tuck into the good things given them with equal cheerfulness and gratitude.

After Headcorn or Paddock Wood the trains stopped at Tonbridge and much the same scenes were here enacted. Before the Headcorn stop had been instituted the wife of the Tonbridge Station Master, moved to pity by the hungry and tired air of the soldiers, had given them everything she could, and her good example was soon followed. Collections were made from civilian passengers in trains or waiting on the platform ; there were actually queues of people waiting to put their offerings into collection boxes. On the first day £25 was thus gathered in ; on the second it had risen to £125. Altogether the Station Master and his staff collected in money a good £1,000. There were milk churns of water all along the platform, filled through a garden hose by the refreshment room tap. Two famous firms gave between them 60,000 cigarettes. Tonbridge like Todgers's " could do it when it chose."

The same sort of thing—the ready sympathy, the improvised food and drink, the amateurs to help distribute it, the postcards given out to the men to tell their people that they were home—was happening at Faversham, at Redhill, at Guildford, in short everywhere

29

where the trains paused on their various ways. Even when those
trains " routed " to London drew quite near to it, the suburbs insisted
on joining in the reception. Among them Penge East deserves
honourable mention. Here again the Station Master's wife was the
first of the ministering angels, with chocolate, fruit and cigarettes, and
volunteers and collections quickly followed. Penge was, moreover,
unique in providing music for the men " to sing them hame to their
ain countree." As one of the earliest trains came through, the band
of the Salvation Army was passing along the road and the Station
Master shouted to it " Why don't you come and play to them ? "
The Salvation Army Captain promptly wheeled his men on to the
platform, and as the trains went through the band struck up a
thunderous welcome. This band, gleaming in blue and red and gold,
paying a passing tribute to war-stained khaki makes, I think, one of
the pleasantest and most touching little pictures of all that stirring
time. Nor was that all for the band took part in a Sunday evening
concert in the goods yard to raise money for the collection. The
waiting rooms were denuded of seats ; the piano of the Station
Master, himself an amateur of the clarinet, was brought down into
the yard on tottering shoulders. A musical Guard took the chair and
sang songs to the accompaniment of a railway clerk ; local artists
were pressed into the service. As a result of all this most practical
enthusiasm, enough money remained over, when all the men in the
trains had been fed, to send fruit and tobacco for eight weeks to the
wounded in hospital at Orpington and Farnborough. It is a little
record to warm the heart, and the clarinet solos of the Station Master
and the songs of the Guard go to swell the murmur of the under-
currents of history.

Finally, there is one postscript that must be added to the story of
these nine days. As we look back on them now and try to remember
what we felt, it seems as if nothing else had mattered or happened in
all the world, except the rescue of our soldiers from their imminent
peril. We recall the gratitude and astonishment with which day by
day we heard of the rising tally of the saved, and that is all. We are
right in thinking that nothing else mattered, but a great deal else
happened. Workaday life went on ; though their thoughts may
have been elsewhere, men and women still went to their offices and
their factories, and had to be carried there. For the railways the

extraordinary was piled on the ordinary. There was a little easing of its labours in the altering or cancelling of some of the train services from the focal point of Redhill, to Guildford, Tonbridge and else-where, and even then other ways of travel, as by omnibus, had to be devised. Apart from that all the work of the great move was simply added to the normal routine. During the time of it the daily suburban traffic was to all intents and purposes unaffected, and the Southern Railway carried 20,000,000 passengers and 6,000,000 tons of freight.

When it was over the General Manager, Mr. (now Sir Eustace) Missenden, addressed a letter to all the members of the staff, and it may fitly end the story : " Now that the task of conveying the B.E.F. on its homeward journey is over, I want to express to you all my unbounded admiration for the way in which this work has been planned and carried out. The long hours and devoted service of thousands of railwaymen and women have enabled this most difficult operation to be brought to a successful conclusion, and I feel sure that everyone of you who has taken part in it will always remember it with pride and thankfulness as I do. THANK YOU ! "

Chapter II

EVACUATION

IN this story there is only one supreme evacuation, that of Dunkirk;
but there are several others, of minor importance by comparison,
which yet entailed for the railways an immense amount of
organisation and hard work. There were plenty of evacuation
schemes that were carried out and there were still some more which
had been planned in case of need and were mercifully not wanted.
The railways had to evacuate people, then in some cases to re-evacuate
them from cities of refuge that had become vulnerable, and finally
engaged in the happier task of de-vacuating them or, in the English
language, of bringing them home. Figures may convey some
faint notion of the number of trains and the amount of work
involved, but there was this additional burden, that in the very
nature of things evacuations too often took place at times of other
and intense railway activity. The first great movement of school
children from London on the outbreak of war naturally synchronised
with the troop movements demanded by the sending of the B.E.F. to
France. In the Spring of 1940 the fall of the Channel Ports did
not only entail the gigantic task of Dunkirk; places once deemed
safe became safe no longer, and that meant more children's trains.
Only a short time after the last British soldier was out of Dunkirk
came the evacuation of the Channel Islands, and that meant for the
Southern Railway both trains and boats.

The evacuation caused by the blitz had by comparison no special competitor, though the railways were up to the pin of their collar. And then soon after D-day—and the work did not end with that day itself, but grew if possible still more strenuous in its sequels—came the flying bomb, and yet another move from London and its suburbs. In short, evacuation constantly played, to all appearances, the part of the last straw, though it never broke the railways' back. The more one studies this story the more one is struck by the fact that the railways can always take a little more in their stride.

Many of the evacuation schemes had been very carefully thought out beforehand. After Munich the red light had been all too visible. If some of us perhaps went to sleep for a while safely and happily in our beds, authority did not. Many meetings were held both in London and elsewhere, and schemes were prepared for the evacuation of the civil population from London and some of the provincial towns. A proportion of patients in certain London Hospitals were to go elsewhere in order to provide room for the victims of hypothetical air raids. There was a scheme for moving and storing non-perishable foods at various points in the reception areas. There was another for moving meat and butter, stored in warehouses in the Port of London, to the Provinces. Yet a third contemplated the whole of the Government Offices leaving London *en bloc*, but this was only carried out to some extent and piecemeal. One, which was not carried out at all, was for the evacuation of coast towns in Kent, if necessary twelve of them on the same day. All the events expected did not happen, and in course of time some unexpected events did happen, but as far as was humanly possible plans had been made.

Before war actually broke out some of these plans had been put into effect. It was on August 31st, 1939, that evacuation was decided on and the next morning it began. That involved not merely the moving of women and children from London and its neighbourhood, but from Southampton, Gosport, Portsmouth and the Medway area. The London children, together with those who wished to go with them, assembled at their respective schools and from thence to their allotted trains at various stations. The main termini could not deal with them all; suburban stations were also used, on the Southern Railway Richmond, Wimbledon and New Cross Gate. The London Passenger Transport Board conveyed the children to their points of

33

departure, partly by their road services and partly by a large number of special trains. In the London area alone 5,895 road passenger vehicles conveyed 345,812 passengers to their stations. The movement was largely completed in four days and it may be added that this, which was by far the greatest civilian mass movement ever undertaken in anything like the time, coincided both with particularly heavy freight traffic and with the severest possible strain on ordinary passenger traffic, owing to individual desire on a large scale to get away from points of danger. That danger did not at the time materialise, but it was very generally expected to do so, as we are now inclined to forget, with the very first shot of the war. Nobody then dreamed of a " phoney " war. The world expected a sky black with German planes from the word " Go."

All evidence goes to show that the great movement was carried out with wonderful smoothness and calm. I did not personally see it, but I have seen the much happier spectacle of the exiles' return to London. It went like clockwork. The long row of omnibuses was drawn up by the side of the platform. The train came in and instantly there sprang into action the stewards with their red armlets and the volunteer porters with violet ones. Every passenger in the train bore a label of destination, and in a wonderfully short time they were collected into groups along the platforms. Many of the children were incidentally so small that they must have been born in the country and this must have been their first sight of London. Everybody, down to the smallest child, was perfectly tranquil and unruffled. Now a gate was opened and one group after another marched down the platform and through the gate. " Brown bus for mauve labels " announced a steward, and the bus was soon filled or not quite filled, since it seems that for one reason or another there are never so many travellers as have been expected. It cannot have been more than a quarter of an hour from the train's drawing in that the first bus passed out of the station and then another and another on its heels. And I describe this little scene now and out of chronological order because I am assured that it was the exact converse of those other scenes of more than five and a half years before. Then the buses had drawn up and disgorged their loads, the living loads which in turn were stowed quickly and quietly into the trains, and away the trains went. They stopped on their way every now and then to dump a particular load at a particular station, where there were people ready to receive it, and so on again. The plan had all been thought out beforehand and, which does not always happen in an imperfect world, that which had been worked out on paper also worked in fact.

All those who took part in this first great exodus were not moved to areas on the Southern Railway, but a very large proportion was, and the Southern had to bear the burden not only of the collection in London but of the main part of the distribution. Thus, on September 1st, 2nd and 3rd, the scheme was put into force for the evacuation of the civil population from South-East London to reception areas in Kent and Sussex. Provision was made for 225 special trains, at the rate of 75 trains a day, and over 138,000 passengers. The trains all ran, but the full numbers did not turn up, as indeed they never did. There was, therefore, plenty of room and the task of those in charge was not so much to fit the people in as to spread them reasonably out. There is a passion in a considerable part of the human race, very difficult for the other part to understand, for the closest possible rubbing of shoulders and the familiar simile of " packed like sardines," which to some conveys the acme of discomfort, suggests to others the true jollity of travel.

At the same time, on the 1st and 2nd of September, took place a minor but still considerable evacuation of the Medway towns, Rochester, Chatham, Gillingham and Rainham, to other parts of Kent. That meant another 54 special trains (27 each day), and over 37,000 more passengers ; again all the trains ran and again the numbers fell short. Borstal prison had also to be moved, bag and baggage, on the 2nd and 3rd, and on the 5th thirteen more special trains took 2,600 people from the Belvedere and Erith neighbourhood, again to Kent, which in the following year was to prove the least safe of counties. Also on the 1st and 2nd, 127 trains took 30,000 people, both children and grown-ups, from Southampton and Gosport to various places in Hampshire, Dorset and Wiltshire. And to anticipate a little, eighteen further trains ran from Southampton, Portsmouth and Gosport on the 27th and 28th.

The tale of these first days in September is not yet by any means complete. The moving of meat and butter from warehouses and docks in the Port of London, already mentioned, involved more special trains, and later tea stored in the docks was moved. Then there were irreplaceable treasures of all sorts from the National Gallery, the Tate Gallery, the British Museum and Westminster Abbey. We have now heard how the National Gallery pictures were taken to Wales, first of all to various towns and later to a romantic cave in a disused slate quarry near Festiniog. Sir Kenneth Clark has told us how the last load was still at the door on the point of starting, when the first siren was heard a minute or two after Mr. Chamberlain had finished his broadcast to the nation. In that particular move the Southern was not concerned, but it was very much concerned with another at the beginning of September, that of the departments of the Bank of England. This was to Overton in Hampshire, which thus had greatness of traffic thrust upon it even as did another Hampshire station, Dunbridge, by the creation of the great American depot at Lockerley. The comparison is, to be sure, not quite an accurate one since Overton had always had a Bank of England traffic. It is near the mills of Messrs. Portal, where the paper is made for our bank notes and also for those of several other countries. Now, however, Overton became much busier than ever before, for with the moving of two departments chalets were built close to the station to house 450 people; a great deal of building and other material must be transported accordingly and Overton also had a heavy week-end traffic entirely new to it.

The scheme for the partial evacuation of hospitals, before mentioned, was carried out, the railways all told providing 34 improvised ambulance trains. At the same time plans were being made for clearing all hospitals in a zone of twenty miles along the East and South-East coasts in case of invasion or of sustained enemy air attacks. There were further movements which were not part of any originally planned scheme, but which none the less demanded special trains, namely those of both public and private schools in the London area to new homes elsewhere. Incidentally these temporary abodes became in numerous instances so permanent that for the boys and girls of the time they will wholly represent the school, and it is

The evacuation of children during 1940 was organised down to the smallest detail

SOUTHERN RAILWAY

SPECIAL
ANNOUNCEMENTS

EVACUATION OF
LONDON CHILDREN

Friday, Saturday & Sunday Sept. 1st 2nd & 3rd

The following steam trains are required for the evacuation of children, and will not be available for ordinary passengers

9.15 a.m.	Margate.	2.25	Hastings.
9.26 a.m.	Hastings.	3.30	Tun' Wells.
11.15 a.m.	Margate.	4.15	Ramsgate.
12.10 p.m.	Ashford.	4.20	Hastings.
	Gillingham.		

The Enquiry Office Staff will gladly give further information of alternative services.

Motor coaches met the trains from London to convey the children to their new country homes

round this new home and not the old buildings and playing fields that their school traditions will cluster.

Desultory " trickles " of evacuation continued for some time after the first torrent, but with the war settling down for a while into an unnatural tranquillity there was comparative repose until the Spring of 1940. Then in May the storm broke. Holland and Belgium were invaded, the Germans were sweeping towards the Channel Ports. Dutch, Belgian and French refugees, who had escaped here in time, had to be transported in special trains from our main ports. On the last days of the month began the evacuation of the British Army from Dunkirk. (That, which ended on June 4th, has of course a chapter to itself.) A fortnight later the Southern must undertake another evacuation, involving both sea and land, that of the Channel Islands.

In 1849 the Railway Company had leased from the South Western Navigation Company the steamers running between Southampton to the Channel Islands, and in 1862 it had bought that Company. From that time till June, 1940, including the time of the previous war, those steamers had never ceased to run. In this very June every available boat had been used to transport the potato crop from Jersey and tomatoes from Guernsey. Despite the desperate state of things in France the Channel Islands deemed themselves havens of safety and were expecting visitors to their boarding houses and hotels. Then came a sudden and a stunning blow. On the 19th of June the Government decided to " de-militarise " the Islands, and the R.A.F. and their stores and equipment returned to England. A scheme of voluntary evacuation was announced for women and children, for men of military age who wished to serve in the forces, for other men if there was room for them. On June 28th, the evacuation was over and the de-militarisation, already a *fait accompli*, was announced by the Home Office. On July 1st the Germans occupied the Islands.

Five of the Southern Railway cargo steamers from Dover were used in the evacuation. In all, 8,000 people left Jersey, 17,000 Guernsey and 1,500 Alderney. Some of those in Alderney had originally crossed to Guernsey in the hopes of getting away, but there was then no boat and they had to return. However, on appeal to the Admiralty, they were told to be ready to leave at a moment's notice. The church bells rang on a Sunday morning as a warning, by ten o'clock they were on the jetty with one small suit case apiece, the maximum allowed, and having destroyed their pet animals—a heartbreaking necessity—and let their cattle loose to find food as best they could, they embarked. There was nowhere any panic, or disorder, but at St. Helier all the public houses were shut, no doubt a wise precaution. The crews of the ships had worked hard to improvise seats out of packing cases and generally to make the refugees as comfortable as possible. Shelters were rigged up in alleyways, the officers' quarters were given up to the infirm and to nursing mothers; one captain's cabin held twelve small infants. Many of the refugees had come without any food, apparently expecting to be fed, and the crews gave up all their own food to them. On one ship the cook remained solidly on duty for 48 hours; seamen and firemen were busy all night distributing bottles of warm milk to babies and taking them off the hands of exhausted mothers. Even so more was badly wanted and the captain hailed a passing craft and asked for fresh milk and bread. A tender came alongside bringing not only ten gallons of fresh milk but tea and sugar, jam, cheese and chocolate biscuits. By the time the ships reached Weymouth every scrap of food on board had gone. It was only by the grace of heaven that a brand new baby deferred its arrival till port had been reached. Every man on every ship spent himself in kindness towards these poor people, thus abruptly torn from their homes, and they were pathetically grateful. Some of those who came from Guernsey had never seen a train until they beheld those that were to take them to their places of refuge. These were mostly in the north of England and Bolton, Rochdale and St. Helens must have seemed a change indeed.

When the evacuation was over the Southern Railway were asked by the Government to maintain the service to the Island as long as possible. Surprising as it may sound, some of those who had been officially evacuated chose to return and the service continued without incident or mishap till June 27th. On the evening of that day the Southern Railway mail boat, *Isle of Sark* (Captain Golding), with over 250 passengers left Southampton for Jersey and Guernsey, and her voyage did not lack incident. Jersey was safely reached at 6.30 next morning, the 28th, and the embarkation of passengers was nearly complete when a German plane flew over from the direction of Guernsey. Guernsey was reached without any further alarm at 12.30 with 454 passengers on board, nearly all bound for Southampton, but as the ship was not to sail till nightfall they were allowed to land. By seven o'clock they had begun to come back when three planes suddenly appeared and dropped a salvo of bombs on the pier. They were followed by more, dropping bombs in the town and the harbour and swooping down to machine-gun the streets. Fortunately the tide was out so that the passengers could shelter on the lower landing of the jetty and in fact only one was injured. Meanwhile the *Isle of Sark*'s 12-pounder and four Lewis Guns went gallantly into action, keeping the enemy up in the air and saving the ship from dive bombing. It was a savage and deliberate raid, which killed 50 people and sank a number of small craft, the machine gunning of a life boat on its way from Guernsey to Jersey being entirely typical of its authors. The raid went on till eight o'clock, when Captain Golding, who throughout the hurly-burly had kept constantly in touch with Southampton, received orders to sail as soon as possible. He decided to wait till ten o'clock, however, to give a chance to everyone that wanted to come, and got to Southampton with 647 passengers. The last man to step on board was a Southern Railway Checker, Mr. Prince, who was looking after the loading of two cargo vessels as well as of the *Isle of Sark*, and had to carry on unaided since his fellow-worker was badly wounded. He had no time even to go to his house, but came on board in the uniform he stood up in, with no " portable property " whatever. He was in fact the last man to leave the Channel Islands, for two other ships on the way there were turned back and no British ship after the *Isle of Sark* was seen there for nearly five weary and humiliating years.

In August of 1940 there was another evacuation from overseas in the shape of refugees from Gibraltar, but this is to get too far ahead. Moreover, though they did need some trains to transport them in this country they were the tiniest drop compared with the great flood in June. With the disastrous events in France and attempted invasion a possibility or even a probability, it was clear that many of the places which had been deemed safe in September of 1939 were safe no longer. So there must begin a second

41

great exodus; but whereas the first has been largely to the south and east the whole trend of this one was to the west. The first move was on May 19th, when 8,000 London and Medway children who has been staying near the coast in Kent, Essex and Suffolk were moved in 16 special trains. They were only an advanced guard. On June 2nd nearly 48,000 more children from East Coast towns followed them. That meant another 70 trains, so that in all some 55,000 children had been moved in 86 trains. Eight days later a still bigger move was announced; there was to be a second evacuation of 100,000 London children to Berkshire, Somerset, Devon, Cornwall and Wales, to be carried through between June 12th and 18th. The Southern Railway's share consisted of 42,391 children in 84 trains running from Waterloo, Vauxhall, Clapham Junction, Earlsfield, Wimbledon and other suburban stations. The schools' organisation was as good as that of the railway and the two worked admirably together; but once more parents changed their minds at the last moment, so that the numbers of children never came up to expectations. The first Southern train, for instance, from Vauxhall to North Cornwall, provided for 600 passengers, but actually carried 417 children and 32 grown-ups. And, incidentally, that train was loaded and cleared in—how long will any one guess? Three minutes.

This second move of the children was sandwiched between the two amphibious movements of Dunkirk and the Channel Islands. I have in fact put the three slightly out of their strict order, but the reader will perceive that between them they represented a very nearly continuous operation with no intervals for what could even ironically have been termed repose. There did follow, in a relative sense, an interval, but it was not for long, since with the later days of August and September came the Battle of Britain with its fierce and sustained attack upon London and the London area. This involved a new evacuation scheme and another flow of refugees, not only straining ordinary trains to their utmost capacity but demanding special ones as well. The hop-pickers, for instance, after their annual outing, were invited to travel direct from the Kentish hop gardens to safer places instead of returning to London, and 8,000 of them did so in 15 special trains. During September, October and November 13,500 women and children, registered under the new scheme were, carried westward by the Southern Railway in 23 special trains, and that, too, at a time when the railway's difficulties were enormously increased by constant and recurring damage on its lines, and often by the breakdown of the telephone. By way of illustration, a small boy of seven had the satisfaction of teaching the Station Master of Victoria his business. " Where does the train for Launceston start from ? " demanded the small boy. " You've come to the wrong station," replied the Station Master. " It starts from Waterloo." But the small boy was not to be overawed. " The Station Master at Waterloo told us to come here," he said " A train is being sent to your station to go to Launceston." And Impudence was right and Dignity for once was wrong, for the telephone had been destroyed and there had been no means of telling the Victoria Station Master of the change of plan.

Many of these westward journeys were very long and as autumn drew on into winter they were also cold. So the L.C.C., with the authority of the Ministry of Health, asked the Railway Companies if they could provide hot meals and drinks on special evacuation trains over long distances. The difficulty of getting enough people to cook the meals was very great, but the suggestion was agreed to on condition that the helpers, who were acting as escorts, should also help in serving the meals and in washing up. This was accepted, and on the 6th of November the Southern provided the first of these hot meals, and a very good one it was, for a shilling.

The Battle of Britain ended in a great and decisive victory, but in looking back while we remember the greatness and the wonder of that deliverance, we are perhaps a little apt to forget how critical was still our situation at the beginning of the summer of 1941. The possibility of invasion was not yet over and in case of it the authorities were occupied with a scheme for the evacuation of the civil population from certain areas along the East and South coasts. It was an immense scheme by which 746,000 passengers were to be moved by 988 trains in the course of four days, and, since the avowed and immediate policy was that of " stay put," it had to be prepared with the utmost secrecy. Women and children were to go first, and after an interval in the time-table the rest of the population were, if necessary, to follow. Entrainment stations, reception areas and routes were all tentatively chosen, and there were to be regulating committees set up from representatives of the Railways, the Ministry of Health and the Army District Movement Control Offices. The trains were to have priority of all others, except those carrying troops or military stores and main line expresses. The scheme never had to be carried out, but it meant a vast deal of work. As the tide gradually turned and the enemy attack weakened and our own grew heavier, evacuation dropped away to a casual trickle. This gradual and blessed change may be illustrated by a table showing the number of passengers carried by all the railways under various evacuation schemes between 1940 and 1943.

Year	Number of special trains	Number of passengers (including those carried by ordinary services)
1940	805	485,484
1941	291	131,298
1942	8	6,612
1943	—	3,477

In 1944 there was not as much as a thought of evacuation till nearly half the year was gone. All the superfluous energies of the railways were consumed by preparations for D-day, and all the rest of the world was looking and waiting for it under an ever increasing strain of eagerness. Such enemy attacks as there were were comparatively negligible ; victory was in the air ; the thought of evacuation seemed very far away and most of the old " evacuees " had gone back to their homes. D-day came at last, all was going well and then just a week later there came to London and the Southern counties the first sleepless, puzzled all-night vigil of the flying bombs. Whether proper bombs, as we now call them, or flying bombs or rockets were the least attractive is a question that everybody can determine for himself, but the flying bombs had the shattering quality of a great disappointment ; the danger was universally believed to be past and here it was again.

Two days after the first attack an unofficial evacuation began and people crowded the stations with what they could carry, and waited for trains to take them, their cots and their prams to safety. It gradually became apparent that, however effective the defence, the only real hope of a cessation of the attack lay in capturing the bombing sites, and this could not conceivably happen for some time. When this was fully appreciated there was the old weary work to begin again, and the Government decided once more to embark on the removal of school children and mothers with young children to places beyond the range of the latest peril. The new organised evacuation was not so big as that of 1940, but it was big enough and it differed from its predecessors in one respect ; they had been carried out in anticipation of attack, but this time the move must be made under actual bombardment. The refugee might be comfortably in his train, hoping that in a few more minutes it would roll away with him to peace and quiet, when the siren would wail and the station bell clang out " imminent danger." The total of the officially evacuated was about 200,000, but the number of those who left London as best they could and by the ordinary train service was also very large, and that service had been considerably reduced on account of the vast D-day traffic.

The principle of evacuation was the same as before ; the people were to be collected and shepherded to London, and then conveyed to the various termini. Large numbers left Paddington, Euston, King's Cross and St. Pancras for the Midlands or the North, while on the Southern special trains left Waterloo for the West and South West. Besides those many trains were run direct from Kent and Surrey to the West and to Wales. Malling to Torquay, Eynsford to St. Austell, Hever to Newton Abbot, Sevenoaks to Sidmouth Junction—here are a few instances of this game of " General Post."

Evacuation officially started on July 7th, and on that day, on the Southern, a train from Gravesend, Dartford and Crayford carried 582 people to Victoria to be transferred by road to St. Pancras. On the 8th, soon after midnight, an additional train left Waterloo for the West with nearly 700 passengers, mostly un-registered, and later in that day three more must be run carrying over 3,000 people. The rush was now at its height, and day after day there must be both special trains and additional ones to relieve the ordinary service. On July 11th twenty special trains were run on the Southern for registered evacuees, seven of them direct to the West and the other thirteen bringing passengers to London on their way elsewhere, a total of 12,550 people in all. That was the peak, but a smaller number of special trains continued to run daily, twelve on July 18th, six on the 21st, and so on in smaller numbers. During the latter part of

August the ordinary service sufficed, but there was a small recrudescence of specials at the end of the month. The last official announcement as to evacuees was that 28 of them had travelled by ordinary train on September 8th. By that time the enemy had been driven from his lair and his bomb sites overrun. Instantly, despite several appeals from the authorities, the stream flowed the other way and the return home from the reception areas began.

When the flying bombs had ceased save for occasional and spasmodic visitations, there were the rockets partially to fill the vacant place as far as the London area was concerned. That remained obviously dangerous, but in course of time those who had been evacuated from certain parts of Kent and Sussex were encouraged to go home. The official return began on December 6th from Cardiff to Hollingbourne with 625 passengers, and another Great Western train from South Wales to Reading with 793. A day or two later that game of " General Post " was in full swing in the reverse order with, on the Southern, Reading to Sandling and Exeter to Tonbridge. On the 13th there were four specials, and on the 14th likewise, and so on, but this is " de-vacuation " and, though in itself a pleasant subject, it perhaps hardly belongs to this chapter. When, on the 8th day of May, 1945, the end came at last, the London evacuees poured home in a steady flow, but by that time, and it is a blessed thought, they no longer belonged to the story of the railway in war-time.

Chapter III

DOVER

IF any town in England can claim to have been in the front line, that town is surely Dover. It was heavily bombed, but that was the lot of many other towns. It bore the torturing strain of intermittent shelling for four years, and in that it was unique. *Si monumentum requiris circumspice.* You need only look round you at the gaps in the streets, the still sightless windows, and the battered, almost derelict, look of many of the houses to guess at something of what it endured. There is beyond doubt much worse devastation to be seen elsewhere, but Dover seems to me to have a peculiarly weary and war-worn air. Its normal population of 40,000 was reduced to 23,000 after Dunkirk, and the fact that the loss of life among those that stayed there was comparatively and mercifully small was no doubt due in large measure to the fact that many lived the lives of troglodytes in caves in the chalk cliffs. When the Channel Ports had at length been wrested from the Germans and the long ordeal of shelling was over, Dover bravely hung out its flags and the rest of the world was told by the newspapers of scenes of hilarious rejoicing. But Dover itself thinks that the newspapers, in their desire for what they would call a " colourful " picture, laid on the paint too thick. Dover was too tired to sing and dance ; all it wanted was to rest and be thankful. Only when the strain was over did it fully realise what it had been. The sentiments are probably best described in the words of the Station Foreman at the Priory Station, who had carried on

right through the years of the shelling. When they ended, he said,
" I felt blooming queer."

I will give a few figures presently to show what Dover as a whole
endured, but it is to the port and the railway that I must stick as
nearly as possible. Their stories differ in that the railway's is
continuous, while in that of the port there is a long hiatus. The first
part of it ends with the wonderful escape from Dunkirk, which lasted
from May 27th to June 4th, 1940. After that Dover was taken over
by the Admiralty for purposes of defence, and the port was under
Naval direction. The prospect of invasion was imminent. There
were charges and tank blocks in the tunnels and detonators in the
cranes. Mines for the channel were stored in the Shakespeare
Tunnel, and afterwards transferred to the Lydden tunnel. Barbed
wire was everywhere, there were mines all along the coast. The
Southern port authorities were given ten days' notice to evacuate, and
as far as the Southern was concerned the whole port moved to
Southampton ; Dover remained dormant for more than four years.
Those who know their " Tale of Two Cities "—and I must allow
myself a little Dickens—can hardly think of Dover without remember-
ing how Mr. Jarvis Lorry arrived there after his journey in the damp,
mildewy, mud-spattered Dover mail in order to take the packet to
France. And he comes reasonably pat to my purpose, for was not
the password that he gave to Jerry Cruncher " Recalled to life " ?
and in time, after those four years, Dover was recalled to life. The
first symbol of restoration came in October, 1944, when a fleet of
coasters was chartered by the Ministry of War Transport to carry
ammunition from Dover to Ostend. In November the Southern
Ferry Service started again carrying hospital trains and brand new
locomotives, and, by the way, it was from those most impressive
monsters that mines had been in familiar phrase, " sown in enemy
waters." Then in the beginning of the New Year a leave boat left
Dover—on January 4th—to bring back the first envied leave party.
Four days later there was another from Folkestone. Commercially
the ports still slept, but militarily they were fully alive, and the leave
traffic constantly increased. With 1945 Dover and Folkestone may
be said to have come back into their kingdom. And now before
getting down to the main business let me give Dover's proofs in a
very few figures. In all there fell upon Dover Borough 464 high

48

explosive bombs, three parachute mines, and, a mere drop in the ocean of bombs, three flying ones ; 528 shells fell within its boundaries, but the total number that fell in it and its neighbourhood was between three and four thousand, while nearly 1,800, failing to reach their mark, pitched in the harbour or the open sea. And these shells *were* shells, for it took 40 men seven weeks' hard work to fill up the holes. In the circumstances the casualties seem relatively small, 232 killed, 371 severely and 460 slightly injured. As was said before, the habit of cave-dwelling must have greatly reduced the list. There were old caves in the chalk cliffs, that once perhaps served the romantic purpose of smuggling. Many new ones were added, and in all there was sleeping room for 14,000. But work must and did go on ; people cannot live their lives in caves, nor can they always take refuge during warnings, and of warnings either of shelling or bombing there were all told 3,053. Among them were those given when we were about to shell the enemy, since he invariably retaliated. Figures are in themselves tiresome things, but they seem to me here remarkably eloquent, and if we ever want to talk, as too many of us do, about our own bombs, we may be inclined to hold them cheap " while any speaks " who was at Dover.

The outstanding feat in the story of Dover from a railway point of view must always be associated with the name of Dunkirk —that precise and orderly moving of some 300,000 men who landed at Dover in trains that followed on each other's heels with marvellous speed and smoothness. The blackest day in the story of the railway, not of the town as a whole, was one of the last days of shelling, September 13th, 1944, when the Priory Station was directly hit and several people were killed and more injured. And yet that was a bright day, too, in producing much courageous achievement on the part of the staff.

Those were what to-day are called the " high spots," but the workaday life of the railway was full of danger and of hard work carried through under the most exacting circumstances. The military traffic was continuously and exceedingly heavy ; the civil traffic was complicated by the silting up of goods in the station since the shops of those to whom they were consigned were shut up. In the circumstances it was something to be proud of that it was never necessary to stop goods traffic from arriving in Dover. And that though the line suffered one truly unkind blow in which the enemy had no hand. Everyone who has ever travelled on the line remembers that tall cliff of chalk that frowns down on the line between Folkestone and Dover. On November 27th, in the busy autumn of 1939, the cliff showered down in a spiteful avalanche covering the line, thus making it possible for trains to reach Dover only by the Deal and Sandwich route or by the Chatham line. And as if that was not enough there were two further falls in February.

In some ways the Priory Station has an advantage over most stations for war-time purposes, in that it stands between two tunnels, neither of them very far off. Thus, when there was shelling, rolling stock could be moved into a tunnel, and a tunnel also provided good shelter for passengers. I should have thought that to have a tunnel ready to one's hand at such a moment would have been something to make one profoundly thankful. I should not have wanted telling twice, but taken refuge with complete docility ; but I am told that passengers were sometimes obdurate. Soldiers would often say " Oh, we've seen plenty of this sort of thing," to which the staff's answer was " Very well, but we don't want to have to pick you up," and this in the end generally carried conviction.

I have been reading the diary kept by Mr. Cooney, who was the Under Station Master at the Priory Station, under Mr. Huckle, the Station Master, and it is as eloquent as it is monosyllabic. " Air raids all day." " Bombardment from French Coast." " Shelling." " Shelling. Traffic stopped between Dover and Folkestone "—so it goes on from entry after entry, and month after month, with here and there such a momentous, if strictly irrelevant, statement such as " French ceased fighting." It is at once the most illuminating and impossible document. It shows what Dover endured, and how hopeless it is to tell the story of their endurance without monotony. The first shelling came in August, 1940 ; people from the station ran into the tunnels, and when the Divisional Office at Orpington asked why the trains were delayed, the Station Master replied that he could not run trains through tunnels full of passengers. That is just an illustration of workaday difficulties, and here is another. The locomotive shed is on the sea shore, and when engines were being coaled a look-out man was posted at the top of the coal stacks. As soon as he saw the flash of a gun from the French coast he shouted to the coalmen who rushed into a shelter. Fifty-three seconds later with perfect punctuality the shells would arrive, and then the men came out again, working between flashes.

Just four years and one month after the first shell, the last fell on Dover, and I must concentrate on the last few days in September, 1944, when the Germans, realising that their time was almost up, " stepped up " their attack and fired off everything they could, and particularly on one day, September 13th. When I went to Dover in the following Spring I saw members of the staff at the Priory Station, four of whom had been right through it from the beginning. Mr. Watkins, the then Station Master, only arrived at Dover in September, but came in for the final vicious and despairing attack. The other four were Mrs. Clayton from the Booking Office, Mr. Owen, the Chief Goods Clerk, Mr. Galloway (before mentioned), the Station Foreman and Mr. Savage, a ticket collector, who had passed the age for retirement, but stayed on " for the duration," and never left his gate during the war. True, on being told one day " Bert, your house has gone," he got leave to go and see whether it had ; but finding the house still there and his wife safe under the table, he returned to the Station. Their stories were not only modest, but had a kind of spritely patience which was deeply impressive. One thing which struck me, as it has struck me in other parts of the whole railway story, was the pains that so many of the railway staff had taken to learn first aid and ambulance work, and how well this unselfish enthusiasm was repaid. Mr. Galloway, for instance, has had 27 years of ambulance work, and won all the medals for it that are possible, and the one fact which he allowed himself to speak of with a little pride was that a Sister at the Hospital had watched him doing a job without suggesting any improvement, and that the Hospital declared that no other patients reached them so well looked after as from the Southern Railway. Of shells, " plenty of them " on the bank of the line, of communications down, of signalmen being unable to communicate with one another so that the trains must be despatched by the time-limit system, of the one particular shell " that just missed me on my bike "—of these and many other things for which I have no space, he spoke almost with indifference as all in the day's work, but the fine compliment from the hospital had obviously given a very natural, human, undisguised pleasure.

Now for the 13th September at a little after four o'clock, of which my first witness, if I may so call her, Mrs. Clayton, has a short but dramatic story. She was issuing tickets and had had some experience of doing so during unpleasant times. In a certain dive-bombing raid in 1942 she had lain down on the floor of her booking office, jumped up to issue a ticket, lain down once more and then up again for another ticket, and so on till the raid was over. Now she began to think that the shelling was a little bad, and that intuition probably saved her life, for she had just moved into the parcels office when a shell crashed into the booking hall and, as it was, she spent seven weeks in hospital.

My second and chief witness, Mr. Savage, has a longer story, and I must try to tell it as nearly as I can in his own words, though I cannot hope to reproduce the cheerful gravity—it is the best phrase I can devise—of his narrative. At four o'clock he came on duty as Ticket Collector, and shells were falling, a train was just arriving and many people came off it. To all of them he gave the warning "Don't leave—take shelter." One lady was not to be moved. She said, "It's quite all right," and she hadn't far to go. Twice more he showed her the shelter and she would not go. He then went into his hut when a shell fell in the Station Approach just outside the Parcels Office, and "Crash—everything started falling on top of me." He got up and shook himself and then went with Mr. Galloway and others of the Staff to give first aid. A sailor lay dead by the side of his hut, and in the booking hall the first body he found—there were four others—was that of the poor obstinate lady.

The shells were still coming over steadily and those two, Galloway and Savage, set to work methodically to clear up the case of tickets which had fallen on the floor. Then Mr. Savage collected some bits of wood and a hammer and nails and proceeded to mend his hut. This seemed in the circumstances excessive, even to Mr. Galloway. "For God's sake, Bert," he said, "get under cover." The Parcels staff were less polite. "Bert, you silly old fool," they shouted, "What are you worrying about that for?" But Mr. Savage said " Somebody's got to do it " and went on hammering. On the same principle that somebody had to do it he cleared a pathway in front of the hut, and mopped up the blood in the booking hall. In the intervals of this grisly task he " dodged down between trains " to the shelter to see how the people there were getting on, took them cups of tea and salvolatile, and " asked them if they wanted a song and dance." And all this, though it does not take long to tell, lasted a long time, for many people were in the shelter for eight hours. As I left Dover I had the honour of showing my ticket to Mr. Savage at the barrier, and I felt as if I should like to keep it ever afterwards.

Let me round off this account of Dover with one of a common event there, which I was lucky enough to see, the departure of a leave train in war-time.

The sight of a leave boat arriving is a moving and exciting one for obvious reasons. It is also a striking one, so it seemed to me at least, as an unobtrusive wonder of organisation. Really our people do seem to do things very well when they set their minds to it. The deck looks as full as it can be—there are some fifteen hundred men on board—but before they reach the shore they have been sorted, exactly how I do not know, so that the moment the gangway is down they file along in an endless and orderly stream. Every man has his kit and nearly everyone has an odd-shaped parcel, some more than one, clearly containing souvenirs which it would be intensely interesting to see, from an obvious German helmet in blue tissue paper upwards. He also carries a blanket issued to him for the journey, and as he comes off the boat he throws it into a waiting lorry. In the last war men came muddy from the trenches, but on this boat everyone looks if not positively smart, at least clean and brushed-up.

The stream now flows in a narrow curving course and presently passes two Customs House Officers. These do not seem as interested in the souvenirs as I am. They cast a kind and deliberately unobservant eye on the largest parcels and do not, at any rate when I am looking, enquire into a single one. That mild ordeal over the men pass on to the platform, where a long, long train of Pullman coaches is waiting for them. This particular train is bound for the north, part of it as far as Aberdeen. Each coach has a letter of the alphabet boldly chalked upon it, and each man seems to find his own with perfect ease. He deposits his kit, and mug in hand departs to a canteen for a cup of tea before starting, though he will, of course, also get food on the train.

The whole process is astonishingly smooth and orderly, and astonishingly silent. There is scarcely a sound, except the tramp of many feet along the platform. Not only is there no hilarity but there is only the very smallest buzz of talk ; ten men at lunch in their club would make, as it appears to me, far more noise. The men look well and cheerful, but for the moment at least entirely serious. There is something almost ghostly about the quiet of it all. Were leave parties as quiet during the last war ? I seem to recall singing " Good-by-ee " with fervour when we sailed away from Greece for the last time, but then it was for the last time, and there was no going back in nine days. What did we do at Southampton ? I try to remember and I cannot be sure, but I do know that this silence at Dover was to me and to others with me surprising and unexpected. I hope that the talk began to flow when the train had begun to move, and perhaps some irrepressible spirit produced an accordion. I may be painting a false picture, but I do not think so. It was at any rate extraordinarily different from that which I had expected.

Chapter IV

ENEMY ACTION

(a) IN LONDON

OTHER people's bombs are notoriously less interesting than our own. Sometimes indeed they are almost unendurably dull, unless there is a tacit bargain to the effect that I will listen to your bomb story if you will afterwards listen to mine. Even so we are apt to sit drumming with our fingers and paying scant attention until our turn comes. In spite of this natural and discouraging phenomenon I do not wholly despair of interesting the reader in the Railway's bombs. They are not only on an infinitely greater scale than private ones but in a different category, for they may be said to be all of our bombs. Nearly everyone who has travelled by train in war-time has had personal experience of them. Even if he has been lucky enough not to have them falling round his own train and his own head, he must inevitably recall many occasions on which he has had to find his way, whether to his work or his home, through all manner of difficulties caused by enemy attack, late trains, trains diverted to roundabout routes, improvised bus journeys—there is no end to the list. He has seen plenty of evidence too, his faithful terminus, to which he repairs daily, become on a sudden battle-scarred or gutted with its once stately roof of glass shattered so that it seems like a windowless house staring with blinded eyes at the sky.

Yet any individual passenger has probably had only the tiniest glimpse of the tiniest fraction of the sum total of damage done and difficulties overcome. The appendix of this book will give him some figures which would be inappropriate in a general survey and I shall not deal in many statistics, but here is just one very eloquent fact; between August 24th, 1940, and May 10th, 1941, there were, as arithmetic shows, 252 days, and on 250 of them there were raids on some part of the Southern system. In a familiar phrase, that just shows you, doesn't it ? If one has oneself been stupid or unobservant or unimaginative it is generally a fair inference that a good many other people have been so too. Therefore I shall presume that I am by no means alone in having had the most utterly inadequate notion of what the railway had to contend with. To take one outrageous example, I had often thought and have often heard other people say that a railway line is a narrow mark to aim at, and that to the enemy high in the air above it must appear little more than a streak which he is extremely unlikely to hit. Having thus exposed my own folly and perhaps that of others I must add that the Germans were better shots than I had deemed them. But in any case if a line is comparatively narrow it has in many places buildings on either side of it, and if the line was not hit the buildings often were. To-day we still see the gaunt skeletons which are all that are left of them or sometimes the hollows swept and garnished where they once stood. What I fancy we do not always appreciate is that the wrecks of those buildings may have fallen across the line, covering it with a mass of tangled ruins, that looked as if some malignant giant had laid them there in order that he might enjoy a game of " Spillikins " on a colossal scale.

Then again if a line is no easy target, what of a marshalling yard with its acres of lines, or of a great terminal station with all its surroundings ? Here were targets broad enough, hardly to be missed in those early days when the Germans first penetrated the defences of London. Only the railwaymen themselves, who endured the attack night after night, can know what it was really like from the railways' point of view. All I can say is that having plunged into the records I can at any rate form some very faint conception of it. An engine driver who wrote down in his own words his account of an appalling night on Cannon Street bridge, ended with an expression of his views with which others, he thought, might disagree though he personally adhered to them. " In my opinion," he wrote, " this was a proper nightmare." To read these records is to grant him a genius for understatement.

Apart from any one traveller's inability to take a bird's eye view of the recurring damage on the whole Southern system there is one very particular reason why it was at the time impossible to realise it. That is the astonishing swiftness with which it was repaired. This was due to great technical skill and enterprise and to careful preparation, such as the storing of material ready to hand and the keeping of relief trains prepared for immediate action at different places on the line. More than to anything else, however, it was due to the dogged heroism of the railwaymen themselves, the " all in the day's work " spirit which accepted everything as it came as part of the job which had to be done. Just as the actor says, " The show must go on," or the journalist, " The paper must come out," so the railwayman takes as his motto, " The train must run." Here is one instance taken almost at random from the diary of the Station Master at Waterloo. I have chosen it both for its dry matter-of-fact brevity, with never a superfluous epithet, and for the little outbreak of fine cheerful defiance in the concluding words. Early in March, 1941, there was a heavy raid on the Waterloo area with showers of incendiaries, at once put out by the staff, and several bombs large and small ; sleepers were torn from some of the tracks and traffic had to begin and end at Clapham Junction. Here is the Station Master's summary. " All roads out of service at 9.0 p.m. Saturday. Examination of arches at 8.0 a.m. on Sunday revealed two large craters in arches in Up Main Through and Up Main Relief. Bomb pierced boundary wall and footings on Down Main Local. Up and Down Windsor lines opened for traffic at 9.37 a.m. Sunday. Roads tested and Up and Down Main Locals opened for traffic at 3.15 p.m. Sunday. Crane arrived 1.50 p.m. and two sets of way beams put in on Up Main Through ; two other sets unloaded and Down Windsor Local opened at 5.0 p.m. Sunday. Normal working of all steam services from 11 a.m. Sunday. Down Main Through opened at 9.8 a.m. Monday. Crane arrived 8.54 a.m. Monday and way beams, etc., put in Up Main Relief. All squared up by 3.15 p.m. and absolutely normal working resumed at 4.0 p.m. Monday. Now beat that, Mr. Hitler !" A little more than two months later Mr. Hitler gave up the unequal contest.

If that strenuous week-end had stood by itself it would have been stunning enough, but that was only an incident. If it was not one thing it was another; if one place escaped another was hit. Two days after that very week-end there was trouble further down the line in the Portsmouth area, and so it was day after day. The labours of Sisyphus were nothing to that of the railwaymen. If the line from A to B was clear, B to C was blocked; when that had been cleared there came a delayed action bomb near D. It was a matter of beginning again and over and over again. To sit in an armchair and read about it is to feel something of the intense irritation which had to be bottled up and was the least part of the trouble. I have called the railwaymen dogged. It does them no kind of justice, but I can think of no better epithet for that indomitable spirit that kept pegging away and even saw a grim humour in it all.

Here is another extract representative of many others. I have chosen it because when I first read it it impressed me as a perfect illustration of the saying that "Life is one damned thing after another." This one comes from the Station Master at Victoria. It relates the events of one of the memorable nights of bombing, exactly as he set them out, with an admirable economy of words :—

	Air Raid Warning 9.5 p.m. 16th April.
9.50 p.m.	Line blocked by Brixton, pending search.
10.15 p.m.	Line cleared by Brixton. 10.4 p.m. to Orpington left.
12. 2 a.m.	17th April. Parachute reported on line near Ebury Bridge.
12. 4 a.m.	Two loud explosions and glass fell from roof, and windows blown out Central Box.
12. 8 a.m.	Fire at Grosvenor Hotel. All lines blocked Central Section.
1. 0 a.m.	Fire at Gasometer, Battersea Park, reported.
2.30-3.0 a.m.	Incendiary bombs dropped on Station and extinguished.

2.35 a.m.   Westminster Council reported H.E. bomb and mine
            in close vicinity to Ebury Bridge.
2.40 a.m.   Incendiary bomb fell Battersea Park Station and
            extinguished.
2.40 a.m.   Office lighting failed.
3.25 a.m.   Bomb reported on Up Main Eastern Section.
3.30 a.m.   Gas supply failed.
3.45 a.m.   Waterloo Auto 'phones failed.
4.55 a.m.   Raiders passed.
5.10 a.m.   Signalling failed both Sections.
5.40 a.m.   D.A. bomb between Down Relief and Down Main
            Eastern Section, opposite Sub-Station. All roads
            blocked both Sections.

There is a pleasant touch of irony in the " Raiders passed " amid
all those successive catastrophes. There seems to be nothing else
that could have happened.

> " Thy hand, Great Anarch, lets the curtain fall,
>   And universal darkness buries all."

Nevertheless, Hitler could no more beat Mr. Bridger of Victoria
than he had Mr. Greenfield of Waterloo.

From September, 1940, till May, 1941, the Germans made a
sustained and in many cases indiscriminate series of attacks upon
this country. Some of them were not indiscriminate ; that upon the
railways was clearly deliberate and was made in the hope of putting
them out of action and so disorganising the war effort and the national
life. In the summer of 1944 the railways also suffered much, though
not so severely as in the " blitz," from the fortuitous shafts of the
flying bombs. In trying to present any kind of picture of these
two periods the greatest difficulty is perhaps that of elimination.
There is an overwhelming mass of material and the only hope lies in
concentrating on certain places and certain unforgettable dates. As
to the places, I must of necessity write chiefly of London, and in
particular of Waterloo, which is the headquarters of the Southern,
though, as has been said, the bulk of the offices were in war-time
moved to Deepdene. Other places will, of course, come into the
story, but in order to keep within bounds, the London material,

which is very full, must be allowed largely to exemplify what was happening elsewhere.

As to the dates, there are certain of them that stand out, such as that of the great fires in London of December 29th, 1940. Most people who have had experience of the blitz remember vividly enough their own experiences on some particular occasion which they talk of as " That Sunday night," but they have grown vague as to the precise dates and are even inclined to blend the events of two or three nights in a confusion which not the longest and most hopelessly rotatory arguments can ever disentangle. The best I can do is to take some peculiarly memorable nights in the story of the railway and the reader, in being reminded of them, may be able to attach to them his own personal and poignant memories.

Everybody remembers the first siren on the first day of the war, how we all retired obediently to our shelters with our dogs and our cats, how nothing whatever happened, and we came out again.

As regards air attack it may be said that nothing continued to happen for about nine months. Then, in June of 1940, were heard the grumblings of the coming storm. As far as the Southern Railway was concerned the first blow fell on June 19th, on the Engineer's Works at Redbridge, near Southampton, where a large quantity of sleepers was destroyed. On July 10th a train was bombed near Newhaven, the driver being killed and the guard injured. Plymouth Friary, Fawley (Hants), the Coast lines near Shoreham-by-Sea, the Kent lines, the Isle of Wight, the Isle of Portland—attacks became more frequent and widespread, leading up to the raid on Malden Station on August 16th, killing staff and passengers and putting the Up and Down main lies out of action. Two days later an unexploded bomb at Hook sent trains for Salisbury and Exeter meandering round by Southampton. On the 25th the defences of London were first definitely pierced; there was a fire in Wood Street in the City, but the terminal stations were untouched, though bombs at Feltham, Staines, and Kingston affected the traffic. Next day there was a false alarm of gas and in the succeeding days there were bombs in the neighbourhood of Waterloo, but still the tempest delayed. At first passengers at Waterloo had gone with complete docility to the shelters at the sound of the Alert. By the time the first few days of September were past they had grown used to it and treated it casually enough, walking about with apparent indifference. Then came the night of September 7th, our first memorable date, and there was no more doubt as to what an air raid was really like.

Those who lived near London will remember how they watched, speaking low like people waiting for the breaking of a thunderstorm, the red glow in the sky along the line of the river. Twelve fires had broken out near the Tower Bridge, and by the light of them a man read his evening paper on Wimbledon platform. The shelters at Waterloo were full of people taking refuge, and at 5 a.m. in the morning they were told that all traffic from Waterloo had stopped, and dispersed to find their way home by tram, by bus, by Underground, or as best they could. With the light came the counting of the cost. A bomb had fallen on the track at Juxon Street, close to Waterloo, and made a crater over which hung suspended the metals of three roads otherwise untouched. The piers of the arches beneath were completely gone. Beneath another road, the Up and Down Windsor Through, the arches had shifted off their piers and were hopelessly cracked. Two local lines could be used for vans, but not for passenger trains, and the Down Main Through road was bent. The standstill was complete.

That was not all; the other terminals had not escaped. At Victoria the signalling supply current failed, and hand signalling had to be resorted to. A bomb killed a driver and injured two firemen, as also some civilians. London Bridge had had fires and H.E. bombs, and early newspaper trains had to start from Victoria. There was no station current ; the station was partly closed. At Holborn Viaduct an unexploded bomb fell in the street near the Viaduct, and all lines were blocked till 7.30 a.m. in the morning.

Charing Cross itself was unscathed, but much of the traffic coming to it from Kent, and running roughly parallel with the lower reaches of the river was naturally disorganised. Of the trains that got through nearly all had had some adventure and the driver and fireman, A. Goldsack and A. Robbins, on the 7.16 from Ramsgate, had been tried in the ordeal by fire. They had had bombs ahead of them, behind them, and on both sides of them ; they had frequently had to leave their engine and lie down flat on their faces, and get up again when that particular peril was momentarily over. To round off their evening an oil bomb fell on the tender of their engine and they put it out with the engine hose. They brought the train safe in to Charing Cross, themselves as black as niggers, and were then ready and anxious to take an engine to Cannon Street, but the Stationmaster thought they had done enough and would not let them. It so happened that among the stranded at Charing Cross was an R.A.F. officer who was engaged in technical work on bombs. " I can only say," he remarked to the two men, " that you have more guts than I have." It was a compliment worth having.

Let us return to the story of Waterloo, which was now completely closed and could not be re-opened for passenger traffic until September 19th. The concourse (the technical term for what I should have ignorantly called the platform) was as Tadmor in the wilderness as far as passengers were concerned, but heaven knows there was plenty to do without them. The bombing went on steadily, and by the 10th Hungerford Bridge, Waterloo Bridge, and Nine Elms had all been hit. The Up and Down Local lines had been available for traffic, and on the 13th down came a bomb and put them out of action. The mails had been silting up and by the 16th there were 5,000 unsorted bags of them. Those that had been sorted were sent by road to Wimbledon, Esher and Woking. And then to go back a little, there was the question of the paper trains. With Waterloo impossible, it was intended to start the night newspaper trains from Clapham and staff and barrows were sent there by road. Promptly a bomb dropped at Clapham Yard, and that would not do. The papers were then carted to Wimbledon and sent from there, but by the morning of the 9th that would not do either, for the road was blocked. Surbiton was now the nearest hope, and to Surbiton paper, staff, barrows and all were carted by road in weary procession.

Meanwhile, there was the crater in the line at Juxon Street, which the King had come to see on the 9th. For fifty-eight hours it was impossible to attack it, owing to bomb damage on the line. Then the crane arrived with trucks of timber, and there came two hundred soldiers who began to fill up the crater and shore up the arches beneath with 18-inch baulk timber. Misfortunes did not come singly but in droves. Before the Juxon Street work had been completed, came another crater, this time by Doulton's works. A bomb dropped on an arch on the Up Main Local line, and made a hole a foot in diameter right through the arch. That was on the 20th, and the nights now run so fast into one another that it is hard to disentangle them or say which was the worst. The 23rd was, at any rate bad enough, and poor Waterloo, only restored to life four days before, woke to find no points and no signals working. There was, however, one cheering piece of news; the crater at Doulton's had been mended. A later message received at Waterloo suggested a doubt as to the track, but it was decided that such risk as there was must be run. Those who know "The Wrecker" will be reminded of a scene in Norris Carthew's experiences as a railway worker in Australia. "The Commandant of the post would hastily review his labours, make (with a dry throat) the signal to advance, and the whole squad line the way and look in choking silence or burst into a brief cheer as the train cleared the point of danger." Was there, I wonder, some such feeling as the train from Weymouth drawn by the mighty "Lord Nelson" drew near the dangerous place? At any rate, the road held; it sagged twelve inches where the hole had been, but it held.

While all these things were really happening there were one or two others which did not happen at all, and to-day may be introduced as lighter relief, but which then added to the sum of anxiety. This war has been much less rich in rumours and the busybodies who spread them than was the last, but there were rumours and they had to be probed. On the night of September 16th, for instance, lights were said to be seen flashing signals to the enemy from works near one of the terminals, and the police were called in. They went to examine them and found nothing in particular. On the following night the small hours of the morning at Victoria were relieved by a game of "Russian Scandal." At 3.30 a.m. came a message from Brixton, passing from box to box, "Germans landing by parachute, also dropping magnetic mines eight foot by two. These must not be touched or approached." At 4 a.m. Redhill was told of it, and declared they had heard of the mines but not of the Germans. A quarter of an hour later there was a telephone message to Chatham Control. They had heard from Orpington of the mines but denied all knowledge of the German soldiers. They had sent the message to Sole Street to be passed on through signal boxes. Another ten minutes and Redhill telephoned again that the news of the mines came from the War Office, and there the story ends. Somewhere presumably an imaginative signalman had added the parachutists " to give verisimilitude to an otherwise bald and unconvincing narrative." They had no more existence than the Russian soldiers of the last war who had been seen passing through our stations with the snow on their boots.

I have tried to give some sort of general picture, partial, spasmodic, and rather breathless though it be, of the early days of September, because they were the days in which the raids and the tremendous task of tackling them were new. The story of September by no means ends with them, for the 25th was a bad night and the 29th a really terrible one, but I shall have to skip ruthlessly over them. After that last raid there were so many lines blocked in Surrey (incidentally there was a landmine at Merrow Siding) that Paddington was prayed in aid for West of England passengers, though it was not actually needed, for the Engineers got the lines cleared in the nick of time. October was little better at Waterloo. On the 8th four H.E. bombs sailed over the station so near that all the passengers on the concourse fell simultaneously on their faces. On the 13th came a direct hit at Nine Elms Yard, with a huge crater and eighteen trucks piled fantastically on the top of one another.

On the 14th there was a direct hit on the Power House at Durnsford Road, Wimbledon, destroying one of the chimneys, putting half the total number of boilers out of action, reducing the capacity of the station by 50 per cent. A hundred and twenty-seven days of repair work were needed before full power was restored, so meanwhile as many trains as could be operated had to run at a reduced speed. Many a daily-breader must have cursed the sudden dilatoriness of his daily train without knowing the reason for it.

Then, to return to Waterloo, on the 17th there befell an event superficially less dramatic than many others, but from a railway point of view infinitely trying. A bomb knocked out all the automatic signalling. There was not a signal or a signal telephone from Waterloo to Loco. Junction, so that Waterloo had no control of anything within two and a half miles of the Station. Hand signalling must be used, and for this the Station Master had nine competent men, but they were shunters and must be used for shunting, so he was dependent on amateurs—some soldiers and fourteen of his own staff with no previous experience, who had to play a sort of nightmare game of follow-my-leader with their flags. Later on there were to come days possessing for the outsider far more fiery and horrific qualities, but the considered judgment of the professional is that this was the worst.

November saw a bad raid on the 5th, and on the 7th a worse. The nights of the 11th and 12th were actually quiet, but by way of compensation a rainstorm flooded some of the station buildings as much as four inches deep. On the 9th Waterloo came in for yet another turn. A bomb flooded the Waterloo and City Railway and cut off the main water supply from Waterloo Station. Among the debris of the Waterloo-City line a delayed action bomb was said to have been found. The police were told, preparations were made to evacuate the General Offices, but when the experts approached with cautious steps they found the bomb was a revolving cowl blown from a chimney—a welcome little piece of comic relief.

The scene must now be shifted temporarily to London Bridge on the night of December 9th, when an enemy landmine came down by parachute. It did not go off but mysteriously festooned itself round a signal box close to the station. A bomb is a matter for the Army, but a landmine on an apparently perverse principle for the Navy, and a message was sent to the Admiralty accordingly. Meanwhile, the station was entirely evacuated, only the Stationmaster remaining at his post. The two signalmen perfectly understanding their extreme danger, stayed in their box for two hours in order to clear the line. With the morning light arrived two young naval officers, who inspected the mine and then came back to the station. The senior of them wrote down the course he proposed to take in order that if he did not come back somebody else should be left possessing at least the negative knowledge of what not to do. Then, bidding his subordinate stay behind, he set out again on his walk down the platform, his steps making the only sound in that ghostly station till they died away and those left behind waited in complete silence. Presently the steps were heard returning; the mine had been made harmless; the station was re-opened, and of all the crowds of daily travellers that poured in by their daily trains not one knew anything of the deadly drama which had lately been played there. If that mine had exploded, London Bridge Station would for a long time for all practical purposes have ceased to exist.

The bombing year ended with the famous fire raid of December 29th, which so devastated the City of London and on this night London Bridge was in the centre of the picture. At six o'clock came the yellow warning, five minutes later came purple, and at 6.9 red. Half an hour of waiting and then showers of incendiaries over the station and forecourt. The fire squad with other members of the staff helped by police and troops put them all out, but meanwhile large business houses in a street nearby caught fire, and the flames spread towards the station. They might have been kept away by the firefighters, but a bomb had hit the water mains and the water failed. The Fire Brigade and the Station Fire Squad tried to get water from the river, but it was low tide and not till 12 o'clock could any effective pressure be obtained. By that time it was too late; the fire had a firm grip and was beyond control. A quarter of an hour later a large factory collapsed in flames on the line, and it was feared that the fire might reach the timbers of the railway bridge.

This was prevented by the water from an engine in the station used through a stirrup pump. That was one bright spot; so was the fact that empty stock was successfully moved into safety. Through the timely moving of all save those who could directly help there was not a single casualty, and most wonderful of all, the train service, though curtailed, never wholly ceased to function, for the trains from Charing Cross and Cannon Street still ran from a single platform. But the material damage was very severe, including the offices of seven departments entirely wiped out.

Cannon Street and Charing Cross each had their incendiaries on that night and extinguished them. Holborn fought for hours and fought successfully against a fire almost touching the track; but Waterloo had a hard time, with many incendiaries, the roof on fire, a rubber factory cheek by jowl with the station blazing furiously. An A.A. shell unwittingly contributed by damaging cables, telephones were unusable, points had to be worked by hand, many lines were blocked. One train at least could run ; by a peculiarly grim jest it was the Necropolis train, which was protected from a delayed action bomb by screens of coal trucks.

Nevertheless, by the 5th of January normal working was restored, but not for long. The gods or the Germans had by no means finished with their malicious jokes at Waterloo's expense. It was at half-past five in the afternoon that the trains were once more pouring out like clockwork. Less than four hours later, at 9.20, a bomb fell right on the station and shook it to the roots. The offices of the General Manager and the Deputy General Manager were totally destroyed. The Underground lifts were smashed ; the entrance to the Underground choked with debris ; much glass was shattered. But there was only a single casualty among the staff. A ticket collector jumped so high in the air that he sprained his ankle in coming down again. Finally here is a little story of this time, which is either evidence of the activities of sinister and filmy German spies or an odd little coincidence, as the reader pleases. On the evening of the 9th, President Roosevelt's special representative, Mr. Harry Hopkins, arrived by special train at Waterloo. The train had barely left Vauxhall when an enemy plane dropped thirty incendiary bombs in its wake and set fire to the track.

The months went on and there was always something ; but it is characteristic of the cheerful, defiant spirit in which all was endured that the records show as the notable event in the month of February not a bomb but a concert. This, the first of a regular series for which Morley College was responsible, was held in Arch No. 258, the public air-raid shelter. And this is perhaps a good place to break off the story for a moment and say a word as to these shelters in the arches below the station.

It is a truly wonderful place, or rather a series of places. It is almost an underground city, for one white, gaunt catacomb opens into another and the sightseer is soon utterly lost ; he feels rather like a stage army that marches round and round the same place. Most assuredly he is not doing that, for in this hidden domain, over which Mr. Greenfield ruled supreme both as Station Master and

Chief Warden, there is room for 6,500 people, and at times of particularly heavy raids it was filled to capacity. Of them a certain number, about 500, were residents, bombed-out families who had lost their homes, and the rest were temporary refugees. The residents were provided with bunks, and I saw one great hall which alone had housed 300 of these bombed-out families. Here and there out of the big rooms there open comparatively small ones ; these three or four families would appropriate by squatter's right and settle down with odds and ends of their own furniture. They are all gone now, in some cases no doubt much to their regret, for the shelters were closed on May 7th, 1945, and to-day all is empty, swept and garnished, but when I was there there were still traces to be seen of the prescriptive troglodytes—the little pieces of worn linoleum they had laid down on the floor, and a few chairs scattered among the bunks.

The great extent of the catacombs is broken up by blast walls of brick, built to minimize any possible disaster, and the whole place is lighted by electricity and air-conditioned. I chanced to be there on a day of sweltering heat, and the air was wonderfully fresh and reviving. Besides the public shelter the office staff had a shelter of their own, with tables and telephones where they could carry on during alerts, and there is one long room, once full of telephones, where the Headquarters staff at Deepdene could come at a moment's notice in case an invading enemy should draw too near to Dorking. This had been prepared before the outbreak of war, but the organising of the public shelters began with the blitz, and took several months to reach its ultimate state of achievement. To-day it is a little hard to imagine this empty, echoing, ghostly city of refuge once full of human beings. Yet if anyone needs any spur to his gratitude that it is all over this is the place for him ; he seems to be taking part in a service of thanksgiving in a subterranean cathedral.

Now to return to our narrative. March 8th produced a bad raid, but its results and how they were overcome have already been summarised in a document ending, " Now beat that, Mr. Hitler," and I shall certainly not try to beat that. The 19th and the 24th were bad nights, but we must make a big skip to the 16th-17th April, which was one of the unquestionably memorable ones, and here Charing Cross must be allowed to steal the thunder of all the other stations' bombs with the story of the landmine. It may be called that for short, but the mine was but the dramatic culmination of a complex series of incidents which must be set out as far as possible in their chronological order.

The night's events started at 1.50 a.m. with an H.E. bomb on Charing Cross Hotel, and at much the same time about a hundred incendiaries fell on or about the station. There were fires everywhere; three trains were alight in the station itself, and a fourth on Hungerford Bridge. With these various troubles the fire fighting staff wrestled undaunted. They had, fortunately, a Coventry Climax Trailer Pump, which had been " warmed up " in anticipation at the first siren. All the lights had gone out and the men had to climb on to the roof of the burning trains to tackle the flames. Yet by ten minutes past three all these fires had been put out. Before that, however, when things seemed almost past their worst, some time perhaps between 2 and 3 o'clock, the real fun began. Porter Gillett remarked to Mr. Bassett, the Stationmaster, as if he were reporting the most ordinary circumstance, " I've just tripped over a landmine, sir." Mr. Bassett thought at first that this was a joke, possibly not very well timed, but he soon discovered that it was not; there the landmine was. Its parachute was entangled in some ironwork on Hungerford Bridge, and there it hung unexploded, and quite close to a signal-box with the signalman in it.

As if this was not enough, Mr. Bassett noticed almost at the same moment smoke and flames underneath No. 4 platform. Clearly the staff could not cope with this as well as the other fires, and outside help must be sought; but the telephone was out of action, and the Stationmaster called for a volunteer to go for help. Gillett, who had found the mine, said he would go and set out, with the raid still in full blast and the Strand full of fires, to fetch the Westminster City Fire Brigade. He stumbled and tumbled over debris, and three times fell prone, but he gave his message and the Brigade promised to come.

The fire under No. 4 platform was extremely hard to get at, and, despite all that could be done, was creeping slowly and steadily towards the landmine. The danger was so imminent that Mr. Bassett was told to evacuate the station. In his own words, " I said to my

chaps, ' I have orders to evacuate ; what are you going to do ? ' "
" Carry on, sir," they all replied. Carry on they did, most gallantly,
but at half-past four the water failed and now the flames were licking
their way faster towards the mine and drew near the signal-box steps.
All this time the signalman, Briggs, a man of 67, with 52 years' service,
though warned of his extreme peril, had stuck to his box. Now,
an inspector shouted to him, " Bill, you've got to come out of it."
He came out, and being told to be careful of the landmine, dismissed
it with a single magnificently contemptuous dissyllable. " There
are two more incendiaries on the bridge," he added, " and I'm going
to put them out before I go back." This he calmly did, and on being
asked by Mr. Bassett if he felt all right, answered, " I'm all right, sir,
but I hope we don't lose the old box." The old box was not lost,
for the Westminster Fire Brigade had kept its word and arrived.
They played on the fire from the Embankment and put it out at
last, when it was some twelve feet from the landmine.

While these things were happening on Hungerford Bridge two
more had happened at the other end of the station. First, more
incendiaries had fallen on the Hotel, and the fresh fire was being
fought by the staff, the R.T.O. and his men, some Home Guards,
and three brave and invaluable volunteers, two Canadian soldiers
and a British airman who happened to be stranded at the station and
declared that all the thanks should be on their side for so interesting
a night. Secondly, a naval officer, Lieutenant Giddins, with three
naval ratings, had arrived from the Admiralty to deal with the landmine. That officer was entirely determined as to what was to be done;
everybody must retire to a distance of 400 yards from the mine.
There was no help for it and the fire fighters, having half subdued
the flames, had for the space of an hour and a half to look on grudgingly
and see them regaining their hold ; the hotel must burn. Lieutenant
Giddins then told the three ratings to keep at a distance, shook hands
with those on the platform, and went forward alone to look at the
mine, armed with a piece of looking-glass from the Stationmaster
and a bradawl lent by the Strand Corner House, since all the Engineer's
tools had been destroyed. Having lain down on the track to examine
the mine, he came back saying that he " thought it would be all right,"
but that he must first communicate with the Admiralty, and there

A landmine dropped from a German plane on the night of December 12th, 1940. It came to rest at the foot of London Bridge signal box without exploding. The Signalman carried on

One bomb made this crater at Malden, interrupting trains to the West of England

A bridge over Southwark Street was hit and collapsed on the night of April 16th–17th, 1941

The signal box at Tulse Hill Junction, wrecked in the blitz, April, 1941

being still no telephone, he walked there and back himself. " Oh, it just happens to be my job," he said in answer to a sympathetic remark. What did worry him, he admitted, was that his own home had been bombed during the night and he had had no news. He then went to work and by 10.30 a.m. he had drawn the landmine's sting. Soon after four o'clock it had been taken away. It weighed 28 cwt.

So ends the story of this unforgettable night during which all quitted themselves like men ; to which no comment could add ; from which all but the simplest language must detract. It is in itself one long, splendid and continuous purple patch. The most exciting drama of the night was unquestionably at Charing Cross, but the tragedy was at Blackfriars. Here either a landmine or a very large H.E. bomb dropped in the very centre of Southwark Street Bridge, so that the rails fell through the crater like a waterfall, curving down on to the road beneath. Just before this had happened the raid was so heavy that seven men who had been flagging trains and working points took cover in a Military steel shelter protected by sandbags some twenty yards from the bridge. By great misfortune they had not had time to shut the door, or, at any rate, had not fully shut it, when a bomb fell and they met the full blast. They were terribly burned ; three were killed instantly, three died later in hospital, only one of the seven survived to recover slowly from his injuries.

The whole of the Southern Railway terminals had their share of hard knocks which were faced with the usual courage. On the morning of the 17th five of them, Waterloo, Victoria, Charing Cross, London Bridge, and Holborn Viaduct were closed to traffic. Waterloo had been almost surrounded by burning buildings, and its signal-box was closed for an hour while the staff fought their own considerable showers of incendiaries. It was without gas, water, and electric light—all put out of action by bombs, and despatch riders took the place of the telephone. The Waterloo and City Railway, which had been reopened in March after being closed in December, was shut once more, and so at Waterloo were the Bakerloo and Morden tubes. Paper trains once more ran from Wimbledon and Surbiton as in the September days. The morning conditions for daily-breaders approached the chaotic. There was a bus service between Clapham

Junction and Waterloo with a queue of hopeful passengers over a mile long, and the road over which it had to pass was in flames and blocked by fire hoses. The journey took most people 3¼ hours from 8 to 11.15. Things were still disorganised when there came another heavy raid on the 19th, with the blocking of various lines as a result. As one small example, fifteen hand signalmen were on duty continuously for twelve hours between Waterloo and Loco Junction and were then withdrawn as they could do no more. Yet by the 26th everything but the Windsor line trains which travelled to and from Clapham Junction was perfectly normal again.

And so we come to May, the month in which the Germans acknowledged defeat in their attempt, to be renewed three years later, to obliterate London from the air, though not without one expiring convulsion of deadly violence.

The night of May 10th-11th is another of *the* dates, and this time Cannon Street shall come first with its story of men huddled all night on the bridge, not merely with bombs falling all round them but with the lively expectation of themselves falling into the river. About 11 o'clock bombs and incendiaries began to drop in showers, and the foreman and a lineman went out into the thick of them to put out fires on the bridge. When they came back they found that two heavy H.E. bombs had fallen by the side of one of the platforms ; the station hotel was on fire—it was ultimately gutted—and so was the station roof. As pieces from the blazing roof were falling everywhere it was decided that the safest plan for the trains standing in the station was on the bridge, and they were moved there accordingly. The safety was emphatically relative, for the bombs were streaming down into the growing fire ; some fell in the river and the splash from one of them went over the signal-box. The men crouched on their engines or took the best available shelter in the tower on the bridge, making periodical dashes out of it to try to put out a fire in the van of one of the trains. After a while even the tower failed, owing to pieces of masonry falling inside it. There was nothing for it but the naked bridge from which the view became ever more tremendous with the wharves and warehouses by the station making one long line of fire beside the water's edge, while the fumes were so thick that it was hard to breathe. As one of the firemen wrote in his report, " It was all rather terrifying being on the bridge with nowhere to go, just waiting for daylight." I should rather think it must have been.

One of these accounts is so admirable a piece of description in its vividness and its modesty that it would be an impertinence to paraphrase a word. So here it is exactly as it was taken down :—

"*Experiences of Driver L. Stainer, Bricklayers' Arms.*

"I booked on duty at 11.5 p.m. and left the Loco Depot at 11.30 p.m. to work the 12.53 a.m. Cannon Street to Dartford.

"On going up to Cannon Street between Surrey Canal Junction and London Bridge, a fire had started over by Surrey Docks and loads of incendiaries were dropped all the way to London Bridge and the City.

"We stopped the engine at Borough Market and the Fireman put out incendiaries. On arriving at Cannon Street, Platform 6, bombs began to drop, then the aspect signal lights all went out, and then some bombs dropped outside the station, bringing clouds of dust.

"A fire had then started at the side of the station, and it then rained bombs and there seemed to be no stopping. The fires were then like huge torches and there were thousands of sparks.

"The smoke from the fires blacked out the moon, and fires seemed to be everywhere, and then the station roof caught alight.

"To save the trains catching fire, two engines, coupled together, No. 934 and 1541, pulled out of Platform 8 on to the bridge. We stopped twenty yards ahead of the other train, and then, after about ten minutes we ducked down on the footplate. We counted three bombs, the last one was terrific, and very close. There was a terrific explosion and our engine seemed to roll ; at first we thought our train had been hit. The debris flew in all directions—we were very lucky. My fireman said at the time, ' Look out—we are going in the drink,' and I said, ' I thought my back week had come.'

"We looked round, and found that the bomb had made a direct hit on the boiler of No. 934 engine, and it had also blasted our train, and turned part of the train over on its side.

" My fireman and myself went to see where the driver and fireman were, and I am pleased to say they had got off the engine in time.

" Then, looking round, we found our train had caught fire, and the fireman with buckets of water tried to put same out, but it was impossible as a strong wind was blowing up the Thames, and the fire got the master.

" I uncoupled my engine from the train, and drew back about two yards, and scoured the engine, and then crossed to the west of the bridge until dawn—watching the fires. It was just like as if Hell had been let loose.

" I am pleased to say there was no one injured and we were all lucky to be alive.

" Every railwayman at Cannon Street was very cool and calm, and all assisted in every possible way under those trying and unique conditions.

" That is my account of the Blitz."

Does anyone want to read, to say nothing of writing, a better one ? " The smoke from the fires blacked out the moon and fires seemed to be everywhere "—that is a sentence, in its pictorial direct-ness, to say over and over again to oneself. That is what George Borrow called " telling a plain tale well."

The driver and fireman of No. 934 had escaped death by a bare minute. They had got out of the engine one on each side, and were finding their way back to the station by the side of the train when the bomb fell and each shouted to know if the other was all right. The long time before daylight was by common consent very hard to bear. " In front the sun climbs slow, how slowly ! "— anyone who has waited for the light in a raid has been in a position to appreciate that line and can remember how many false dawns he has hailed. When to these men on the bridge daylight did come at last they scarcely knew it from the pall of smoke that was every-where. At last the " All Clear " sounded at about half-past five, and as one master of understatement said, " I had a nice headache and felt smoke-dried."

Now to Waterloo, which from bombs and fires combined had

perhaps its worst night of all. At least I should have thought so, but Mr. Greenfield, the Station Master, says that is an amateur's view. At any rate it was not a good night. High explosive, incendiaries, oil bombs, delayed action bombs—here they all are before me in an extract from the Stationmaster's diary, all chronologically set out. Each with its number in a tidy little bracket, and those numbers run up to sixteen. They left the station without gas, water, electric light, and power, with lifts unworkable, and the signal-box dead. All through the night the A.F.S. staff, the Yard foreman, and shunters and the members of the staff who were off duty but volunteered to stop and help ; all worked with never a break, and as far as surface damage was concerned with the most notable success, for the fires were all put out. I must concentrate, I think, on one H.E. fire bomb, which is numbered 15 in a bracket, since it made so disastrous an attack on the Arches below the station. It fell on some premises close to the building department workshop, and the electric light department and started a big fire there. It blew down the doors of these arches into the Lower Road and this opening of the doors helped by the blast of another bomb spread the flames quickly. Parcels vans, motor horse boxes, and the Chairman's car—these Germans have no sense of propriety—were licked up by the flames in no time, and a number of other parcels vans were moved in the nick of time. Thence the fire spread to more arches, the timber arch a ready prey, and the General Stores, and so on to the Bonded Stores Arches, where was a store of wine and spirits valued at £30,000. These burned like a furnace, and the whole of the stock was consumed or made worthless. I have seen on the Railway Company's private film a picture of workmen subsequently digging and delving among the ruins and pouring away the contents of champagne bottles in a foaming flood, a sight to melt the soberest and stoniest heart. Incidentally, in November, 1940, the Blackfriars Goods Depot had been completely destroyed and underneath it was a Bonded Warehouse containing 25,000 cases of champagne, but that time the issue was more fortunate and practically the whole of the golden treasure was saved.

This fire began soon after midnight and for two hours there was no water, for bombs had severed the mains in Waterloo Road and

York Road. Some was obtained from the surface locomotive supply, but by nine in the morning it was pumped dry. Then a supply was found, the catch pits in the Waterloo and City Railway's berthing sidings and there was a pump ; but to get the pump to the water was a problem. By great exertions it was taken through the Waterloo and City workshops, lowered by a crane, and then pushed over the rails to the catch-pits. Thence the water was pumped over a 30 ft. wall and relayed by other pumps to the fire. Gradually the fire in the Lower Road was got under control, but the spirits still flared merrily. The Fire Brigade attacked them from a fire float in the river, but the pressure was very low, every few minutes the water failed, so that the flames from the spirits came bursting from the white-hot arches right across the roadway. It was not till the 15th that the fires in the arches were finally subdued and the evil that they had done lived after them till well into July.

Meanwhile, to go back for a moment, at 6 o'clock in the morning of the 11th, Mr. Greenfield took a walk along the line from Waterloo to Clapham Junction. He was all alone and may have felt like another Wordsworth on Westminster Bridge. It was the most perfect summer morning, but the world was not " all bright and glittering in the smokeless air." Such a pall of smoke hung over London that it masked the sunshine and everywhere there blew fragments of burnt paper from the surrounding fires. Once again five Southern terminals, Waterloo, Victoria, Charing Cross, Cannon Street, and London Bridge were closed, and not only these ; King's Cross, St. Pancras, the Waterloo and City, the Bakerloo, and the Morden Tube shared their lot. Mr. Greenfield had plenty to occupy his mind beside the beauty of the morning, for it was five days before the station could be even in part re-opened. Eight days later nine roads were open for traffic, and by June 4th all but three. By that time Mr. Hitler had thrown in his hand, but his last effort had not been unworthy of him.

ATTACKS ON TRAINS

So far I have been dealing with stationary targets, and in particular stations, but there are also moving targets in the shape of trains and during three years from July 3rd, 1940, to September 4th, 1943, there were in all 58 attacks made upon trains of the Southern

Railway. A train can stop or it can go on, thus making of itself a harder target, but it cannot dodge. In peculiarly lucky circumstances it can take refuge in a tunnel. It is a narrow mark but it can be extremely vulnerable to a low-level attack and nearly all these attacks were made in daytime, when the clouds were exceptionally low. During this war we have taken a sometimes acutely personal interest in clouds and had a dislike to them on grey, wet, stormy days, when their canopy was close overhead and anything might come out of it on a sudden. That was the raider's chance. Either alone or with two or three companions he could escape the coast defences and dash down low on to a train near the coast, drop his bombs or rake it with cannon or machine gun fire and then up and away again. Nor were these swoops confined to the coast, for there was one as far inland as Alton in Hampshire, and another on a train between Salisbury and Exeter. Many of them were harmless, but a number of people were killed and rolling stock and engines were damaged. I will choose two to describe in some detail, one near the coast and one inland, showing how valuable is a knowledge of first aid and ambulance work, and how much can be achieved by one or two resolute and courageous men who possess it.

On a fine, still, summer evening—there was no cloud this time— a train was not far from Deal on its way from Ramsgate to Dover when, as a complete bolt from the blue, machine-gun bullets rattled against the engine. Six German planes roared low above the train clearly and deliberately aiming at the driver (T. Goldsack) and the fireman (Stickells). Stickells drew back for a moment into such shelter as he could find, then went forward to the driver and advised him to destroy the vacuum brake. This was done and the train stopped. The two men then jumped down on to the line, but the driver at once fell ; he had a hole in his chest and was palpably dying. Stickells was himself wounded in the arm, the thigh, and the leg, and as he only discovered afterwards, in the foot also. He shouted that he was not so badly hurt and staggered down the train towards the guard, but fainted. This guard (Sabine) had twice before been on trains that were attacked, in one of which the driver had been killed, and he was fortunately skilled in first aid. He made a tourniquet for Stickells' arm in which an artery was severed and saved his life.

Luckily there were some Marines stationed near, and they came to help. The guard sent one to fetch their doctor and another to the Deal station, where a train was standing, to ask that it should be sent to pick up casualties. Only a light engine came, and so Sabine had to revise his plans. First the Marines made a living chain to pass buckets of water to the footplate of the crippled engine and put out the fire. Next a fresh message was sent for an ambulance to be in waiting. The injured men were lifted into the train on corridor tables for stretchers. The crippled engine was " blocked out," the light engine attached to the back of the train, an order to use the " wrong road " obtained, and the train was drawn back to Walmer. As a piece of impromptu organisation this was a fine effort, and it is pleasant to know that the fireman made a wonderful recovery from his four wounds. Within five days he insisted on being let out of hospital and within six weeks he was at work again.

Another fireman, Fairey by name, is the central figure in my other and more tragic story. In the early afternoon of December 16th, 1942, the train from Guildford to Horsham was attacked by a single Dornier near Bramley home signal. Four high explosive bombs were certainly dropped, but there seem to be some differences in the evidence as to machine-gun fire. Fairey, who saw the plane coming and crouched down under the coal bunker, was positive he had heard machine-gun bullets hit the engine. He was, in fact, the solitary being in the whole train who was not injured. As the plane passed he jumped again on to the footplate and at the moment received part of the blast from a bomb that fell on the bank. He was smothered in dirt but not knocked down. He first made the engine safe and then, single-handed, attended the injured, of whom the guard and the driver were both dying. Fairey was a member of a Horsham first aid team which had gained great fame through the various competitions it had won. Never was knowledge more valuable, for he was quite unaided in his rescue work until six Canadian soldiers fortunately arrived to help. Mercifully, there had been no more than twenty passengers in the train, but of these eight were either dead or dying and every single one was more or less hurt, some of them badly cut, and for a while, until the doctor came, Fairey ranged this field of death and pain all alone. One small incident shows his coolness. He had put a

mailbag under the dying driver's head and amid all the hurly burly
he remembered to ask the Stationmaster to make sure of the bag's
safety. As Jasper Petulengro would say, " I am of opinion, brother,
that that fireman was a regular fine fellow." And he reported again
for duty next day.

Trains could occasionally, as has been said, escape attack by
diving into a tunnel, and a wonderfully snug city of refuge a tunnel
must have seemed at such moments, to say nothing of the impish
satisfaction of baffling the enemy. The layman has perhaps sometimes wondered whether tunnels were used deliberately to protect
rolling stock, and the answer in a general way is—not very much.
Rolling stock was often moved on to branch lines at night, and at
Bournemouth West, where there was stock berthed to the value of a
quarter of a million pounds, the station was kept open all night in
order that the stock might be moved at a moment's notice. At
Dover, when the town was being regularly shelled from across the
Channel, trains became temporarily troglodyte and retired to tunnels
as the inhabitants did to caves. The one great exception to the rule
was, however, the Kemp Town Tunnel at Brighton, where electric
stock was " stabled " at night, first for a trial period of three weeks
in October, 1941, and then regularly afterwards. The stock was
hauled in and out of the tunnel by steam under a series of elaborate
precautions in which red and white lamps and white posts against
the tunnel wall played their directing parts. This practice continued
until May, 1944.

CAVES

The subject of trains in tunnels seems to lead naturally, if by
something of a bypath, to that of people in caves. The community
of Chislehurst Caves has been one of the curious by-products of the
war, and since the Railway ran special trains there it has a right to a
place. In the last war the caves had sheltered TNT ; between wars
came mushrooms ; with the early days of the blitz in 1940 came nightly
refugees, a small number at first, but growing like a snowball till there
was not a vacant spot for newcomers.

It was safety first and foremost that sent them trooping there,
but for many there was the added charm of a communal existence

81

and for a few, perhaps, romance. Unquestionably, the Chislehurst Caves are exciting and romantic places.

> " East, ah, east of Himalay
> Dwell the nations underground."

He must be lamentably prosaic to whom these lines make no appeal, and these caves burrow their way deep, ah, deep into the face of a hill. In peace time we used to pay a small sum to be led through their mazes, hurricane lamp in hand, by a polite gentleman who told us that they had all been excavated by the Druids with no other tools than the antlers of deer. The Druids must have been remarkably ·industrious people, for the caves are very large, and as far as the casual visitor knows, stretch away to uncharted distances. On the whole, perhaps, we cannot quite swallow the Druids, but the Caves are unquestionably very old, and in the roof of one passage there is a fossilized ichtheosaurus to witness if the Druidic gentleman lies. They were originally, it is believed, pits driven horizontally into the hill ; they were in use in the time of the Romans and were still worked as pits not more than 150 years ago. They have a pleasant, airy, equable temperature and they feel as safe as safe can be ; and the community of night birds which gradually came to stay there was by all accounts exceedingly well managed, nor did the owner of the Caves exploit the refugees. In course of time an elaborate organisation came into being, with a barber's shop, concerts, and church services, and many grew so fond of this existence that even at times when the raids had greatly abated they clung to it for its own cheerful and friendly sake.

Very large numbers took their evening train to Chislehurst as part of the day's routine, the time of the train naturally varying with the black-out. I have myself a vivid recollection of my first meeting with them. I had dined in London and was going home on a fine summer night, perhaps in May. I recollect that the only other person in my carriage was a railwayman, and we were having a very agreeable conversation when, as we drew in to New Cross Station, I saw the platform black with people from end to end, four or five deep. " I get out here," said my fellow traveller, adding with a grim smile : " You'll have plenty of company." He was right, for sixteen people, mostly mothers with small children, surged into the carriage. In my innocence I was utterly mystified by this Derby Day influx. It was only when, to my unspeakable surprise and relief, they all got out at Chislehurst and I could expand and feel myself tenderly, that I thought of the Caves.

That was not a time of bad raids and that train load was obviously composed of regulars, for all seemed to know each other. What the journey must have been like in the time of the flying bombs, which was soon to come, and of the rockets, I can only form a faint conjecture. Most of these regulars went by the ordinary train service, but when raids became worse and more frequent again early in 1944, it was arranged to run a special train from Cannon Street every night when the number of passengers demanded it. It ran nearly every night from January to March. The number of passengers varied between 1,500 and 2,500, and as many as a thousand sometimes travelled between eight and nine o'clock. Two thousand was roughly the number to justify a special train. The peak or rush hour depended on the black-out, and the later the black-out the better fun the children no doubt deemed it, and the worse it presumably was for them. A great many people took season tickets and the family expenses must often have amounted to 30s. a week. Whether many of them will ever get used to sleeping in their own beds in their own houses again it is hard to tell. Say what you will, there *is* something about a cave, and some old troglodytes may feel like Sam Weller's landlord in the Fleet, who always made up his bed under the table because he had been used to a four-poster before he came to the prison. The Caves may well have saved many lives, and if not that they saved many wretched wakeful nights of fear and anxiety. In the circumstances it would be very ungrateful not to believe in the Druids.

FLYING BOMBS

Roughly speaking, from the middle of May, 1941, to the middle of June, 1944, the enemy's attack by air abated. Of course, there were periodical recrudescences, some of them both serious and destructive. There were at all times plenty of small and scattered raids ; the sirens were not silent for long, but the whole scale of attack was smaller. For the Southern Railway by comparison with what had been and what was to come those three years or so were relatively quiet, and this story must make a long jump forward to the time of the flying bombs. If the earlier blitz grows mercifully a little dim nobody needs much reminding of that first sudden night which came to damp our D-day spirits—the grinding, whirring flight of the blind beasts, the more frightening from their inhumanity, the ominous silence of the cut-off, the recurrent crump of explosions, the ceaseless and, as it then appeared, futile roar of the barrage. And there was no hopeful waiting for daylight and no relief with its coming. The sounding of the " All Clear " was too often but a bad joke. In the 80 days from June 13th, when the first of them fell— at Cuckfield in Sussex—till August 31st, when the last came from the launching places in France, 8,000 flying bombs reached this country, an average of 100 every twenty-four hours and the tale of their devastation was great.

Only forty-two flying bombs fell on the Railway Company's property, but that number bears little relation to the damage done to property so near the line as to affect it, and the total number of incidents, to use a comprehensive term, was probably between seven and eight hundred. Having regard to the blind and undirected attack the railways suffered at least their full share, and in some respects, such as bridges, it seemed at times that fluking was more successful than aiming. It was a bridge that provided the first outstanding smash. Those who travelled to Charing Cross by their daily train on the morning of the 19th of June, found themselves arriving at an unusual platform and caught a glimpse of something amiss on Hungerford Bridge. What the landmine had failed to do of malice aforethought the doodlebug by blind chance achieved ; it demolished about 100 feet of the up and down local lines and the footpath.

Exactly a week later the General Offices at Victoria had a direct hit a little before two o'clock in the morning, and 17 people, including six members of the staff, were killed and thirty injured. Those six were outside porters who were doing duty as fire guards, and the bomb must have fallen in or very near the room they were in. There was one more of their party of seven who was untouched, and he owed his escape to a curious circumstance ; he seems to have suffered from a mild form of agoraphobia, surely an unlucky ailment for a porter, and disliked anything like a crowd. So he used to spend his time of fire duty in roving from room to room. Just before the bomb fell, he had been on the roof watching a searchlight. As he came down he opened the door into an empty room, and then, hearing a bomb coming, dived under a desk. He heard no explosion, a not uncommon experience with those very close to a bomb. All he was conscious of was that he had not been able to get his legs under the desk and that debris was falling on them. After a while he found himself on his feet again trying to get out of the room through the wreckage. The staircase was unusable and he wandered about in total darkness till he found a liftshaft and climbed down the ironwork. The moment he got out he was anxious to help in the work of rescue, but he was so dazed and shaken that kindly authority sent him to the first aid station.

The material harm done was very heavy—all the offices on the eastern side damaged, some irreparably, together with several adjoining shops and the Grosvenor Hotel, and not one square of glass left in the roof on the eastern side. Fire, too, broke out in the damaged buildings, but was ultimately put out by the staff working most valiantly, though they were handicapped by their trailer pump having been made useless by blast.

Smaller or greater mishaps followed one another in a more or less steady stream, and it is impossible to enumerate them. The Kent, Surrey, and Middlesex suburbs suffered much, as their names constantly recur. Hither Green as one instance was hit twice, first on June 15th-16th, and again on the 23rd, the second bomb damaging the station itself, two electric trains, and a lot of wagons in the siding, and Wimbledon Station was hit—but the list is unending. Those who feel a justifiable local patriotism may like to study the honours list of the thirteen boroughs most sorely tried, not from a railway but a general point of view. It was published soon after one of our Ministers had declared on September 7th, with a somewhat premature desire to please, that "except possibly for a few last shots" the battle of London was over. Here they are in order of affliction :—

Croydon, Wandsworth, Lewisham, Camberwell, Woolwich, Greenwich, Beckenham, Lambeth, Orpington, Coulsdon and Purley, West Ham, Chislehurst, Mitcham.

The doings of one bomb, the doodlebug of Cow Lane Bridge, may be rather more particularly described both because it was so demoniacally and doubly effective and because the repairing of its ravages was to prove an engineering feat. Cow Lane Bridge, not so rustic as it sounds, is a little to the east of Peckham Rye Station. By it the double line of the old Chatham and Dover from Holborn Viaduct to Nunhead is carried over the South London line of what was once the London, Brighton and South Coast. On July 13th, at 7.30 in the evening, the bomb fell close to the down line below and destroyed the permanent way, while the blast lifted the bridge above, demolished the whole of the centre trestle escept for one stanchion, and left the bridge in a precarious state of suspense.

I am much too little of an engineer to describe what was done and shall take leave to borrow from an excellent account in *The Railway Gazette*. " The bridge is of the two-span continuous plate girder type approximately 110 ft. in length, with closely-spaced cross girders supporting wheel guard timbers and timber decking. Except for some adjacent sidings the lines carried by the bridge and those under it are electrified on the third rail. It was imperative that the power supply carried by the undamaged cables should be maintained without interruption, and to this end a temporary timber bridge, in three spans on trestles, was erected on one side of the bridge, and the cables were carefully extracted from the wreckage and transferred to it. In addition, all but one of the broken H.T. cables were jointed and supported in this way."

The old bridge had to be removed, and it was thought that the best way to do this would be to demolish it on the ground level. The Royal Engineers accordingly put charges against the remaining stanchion and hopefully awaited the result. " You must not suppose the dynamiter's life to be all gold," remarked Zero ; explosives can be fickle and one girder at one end of the bridge did not behave as it should and fall clear of the abutment. Much cutting was done by oxy-acetylene, cranes moved the wrecked ironwork into trains, and the train took it away. Meanwhile, a temporary three-span bridge had been designed, " using military-type trestling for the supports and 24 in. by $7\frac{1}{2}$ in. rolled steel joists to carry the tracks, with the whole structure carried on new concrete foundations and the existing abutments." This bridge was put up by means of a 10-ton crane below and a 36-ton crane on the line above, and the entire work from the moment the bomb fell took nine days and a half. To me, at any rate, that sounds almost magically quick.

It was not only London and the suburbs that suffered. A map of Kent shows the whole of that county save for one small bald patch thickly and impartially plastered with flying bombs. Maidstone West Station had one in its sidings which did much damage and killed five people. Ashford, so immensely important a railway centre, which had, considering its status, escaped lightly, was damaged by a bomb that exploded in the air, a fact which leads to a curious and unfortunate event near Rainham. The bringing down of a flying bomb was now and again a Pyrrhic victory. On August 16th, a bomb was shot down ; it fell on a bridge which carries the line over a country lane beyond Rainham Station between Gillingham and Sittingbourne and made a hole in it. Just at this moment a passenger train from Victoria was drawing near, and the bomb fell twenty yards or so in front of it. The driver saw it coming and used his emergency brake, but he could not stop the train before the bridge. The engine was overturned, dragging the first two coaches with it, and eight people were killed and sixteen seriously injured. Some little while before something of the same kind had happened on another part of the line, with a luckier issue. A pilot who had helped to bring down a flying bomb was able to signal to the driver of a goods train so that he could pull up a few yards short of a mass of rubbish thrown across the track.

All the endless incidents, smaller or greater, involved not merely repairs but a long series of diversions and alterations of the usual time-table and a vast amount of what the layman has since the last war called " staff work." Anything in the nature of a railway time-table has a fascination for those who are Bradshaw-minded, and it may please them and may also convey to others some notion of the continuous problems with which the Railway was posed if I set out just one extract from the orders for an emergency service for just one part of the line. It is chosen at random as an illustration, and was issued on July 13th, to hold good till further notice.

A.M.		UP TRAINS		
4.0	Orpington	... Holborn ...	⎫	Diverted via Mid Kent, calling
5.7	Swanley	... Holborn ...	⎪	Beckenham, Catford Bridge,
5.40	Swanley	... Holborn ...	⎰	Ladywell, New Cross, and
6.5	Swanley	... Holborn ...	⎭	London Bridge.
6.11	Bickley	... Holborn ...		Will not run.
6.1	Sevenoaks	... Holborn ...	⎫	
6.21	Sevenoaks	... Holborn ...	⎪	Diverted via Herne Hill, calling
6.41	Sevenoaks	... Holborn ...	⎰	all stations.
6.53	Sevenoaks	... Holborn ...	⎭	
7.12	Bickley	... Holborn ...		Will not run.
7.21	Sevenoaks	... Holborn ...		Diverted via Herne Hill, calling all stations.
7.42	Sevenoaks	... Holborn ...		Terminate Swanley.
7.40	Maidstone	... Victoria ...		Call additionally Bickley and Bromley. Diverted via Mid Kent, running past Shortlands to Blackfriars.

That will have to do as a microcosm of the whole problem. Here are just one set of trains following one another at rapid intervals during only a fraction of the working day. It is a vague, if impressive, sum in the nature of rule of three to imagine the amount of changing and calculating and devising to be done for the whole line and carried to a successful conclusion under continual possibilities of attack.

ROCKETS

After the flying bombs the rockets ; but some future historian of the Southern Railway, groping his way among dusty old files, may be a little mystified by finding no mention of them. The Government said for some time no word about them, and the Press was silent. The Southern Railway was equally discreet even in its own departmental correspondence, and one incautious person was reproved for writing of rockets, on the ground that " officially these do not exist." The irreverent cockney called them " flying gas-mains," and the Railway employed the felicitous euphemism of " happenings," afterwards changed to " an explosion—presumably enemy action."

However, to-day we may call them rockets, and very unpleasant they were. The Southern Railway had, together with the rest of

A chance hit on the Viaduct over London Road, Brighton, by a tip-and-run raider in 1944

don ing— der gate ll dge, e r h the ains inued run. ril, 40

Christmas shoppers were amongst the seven people killed in a local train from Horsham to Guildford in 1942

The ruined interior of Portsmouth Harbour signal box after the severe bombing of January 1941

With Portsmouth Guildhall and the high-level platforms in the background, a damaged
local electric train was broken up on 4th May 1941

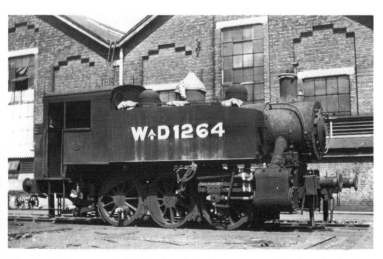

After hostilities, some of the American-built shunters were offered to the Southern
Railway. This moth-balled example is seen at Eastleigh Works

The engine which saved a bridge, May 11th, 1941.   The bomb fell on the cab of the engine

A fly-bomb wrecked one side of Charing Cross railway bridge on June 18th, 1944, and damaged the footbridge

London and the suburbs, its share of them, but except for one calamitous instance, they did it relatively little harm. Various damage was done and lines were blocked by debris for a while, but the trains were soon running again; there were never any stoppages in the least comparable to those of the blitz, and it would be tiresome to go into details.

Only two catastrophes causing loss of life, one small and one sadly large, need be specified. On November 25th, 1944, soon after 12.30 p.m., a rocket fell near New Cross Gate, damaging windows and roofs at the station, signal-boxes and motive power shed and a workshop. Two men, members of the staff, were killed and two women carriage-cleaners, believed to have gone to Woolworths for their lunch, were never seen again. Woolworths at New Cross, as will be remembered, received a direct hit when it was full of people. In the following March there was a horrid disaster in much the same sorely-tried neighbourhood. This was at the Company's flats at Folkestone Gardens, Deptford, near the lines by North Kent East Junction. The damage to the line was trifling, but nearly a quarter of the flats were demolished and 51 unfortunate people killed, including one member of the Railway staff and six staff dependents. Later on the same day another rocket fell at Angerstein's Works, near Charlton Junction, and three members of the staff were killed.

On March the 26th, there was slight damage about 80 yards from the line at Chislehurst, and as far as the Southern Railway was concerned that was an expiring effort and the end of the war in Europe. Not long afterwards the Prime Minister, on being asked in the House of Commons, if he had any news to give as to the V2 attacks, made the historic answer, " Yes, sir, they have ceased."

ENEMY ACTION—BRIDGES AND ARCHES

Demolished	14
Seriously damaged	42
Less seriously damaged	143

MATERIALS USED IN REPAIR OF BOMB DAMAGE

46,500 cubic yards of filling material.
1,904 tons of steel girders.
650 tons of steel trestles for bridges.
109,600 cubic feet of heavy timber to strengthen tracks and bridges.

Chapter IV

ENEMY ACTION

(b) IN THE COUNTRY

This Chapter has already run to inordinate length, and yet I seem only to have touched the fringe of the subject and done the scantiest justice to but a few stations and their staff. There are so many, many more, and only a small fraction of them can have a bare word apiece. I have dipped and dived into their records and found things both tragical and trivial. And is not that characteristic of air raids and the way in which the English people received them ? At one moment they were lying flat on their stomachs in fear of imminent death, and the next they had picked themselves up and were laughing at some grotesque little incident that appealed to them. By way of example take just two of the many suburban stations that all had the hardest of hard times. Herne Hill had bombs in plenty, but it takes more pleasure in recalling how one day it was smothered not with bombs but feathers from the feather bed in some luckless house near by. Penge, in a sadly battered neighbourhood, had a hole through its famous tunnel, right through the earth above and the brickwork casing, but has time to remember the old lady who, recovering from a " near miss," offered the kind porter a penny " to get a piece of chocolate to revive himself."

Then there are the seaside stations—Dover and Folkestone, Deal and Sandwich, Brighton, Eastbourne, and Hastings, Seaford, Newhaven, and plenty more all within but a minute or two of flying time from the enemy airfields, constantly subject to hit and run raids, always liable to have the bomb first and the warning afterwards. Dover has had its finger in so many war pies that it has elsewhere a chapter to itself; but Folkestone, too, was bombed and shelled through the years, though on the whole Folkestone and Shorncliffe stations were wonderfully lucky. The Stationmaster's house was the exception to prove the rule; the enemy had a dozen partially successful shots at it, and with the thirteenth they got it beyond all doubt. Brighton, apart from other considerable railway damage, had its proofs to show in one curious freak of bombing. One out of five bombs that came on a day in May of 1943, fell on the viaduct between Brighton and London Road, near the Brighton end. It entirely destroyed one of the brick piers and left the metals defiantly in position suspended over space. Eastbourne, a regular target of the hit-and-runner, suffered from what was surely one of the bitterest of the raids' little ironies. On the 16th September, 1942, a demonstration of a motor fire pump was being given by an inspector to the railway staff, when a raider flashed over. The inspector and several of the staff were killed and the pump wrecked.

Then, a little inland from much tried Dover, there was Canterbury. Canterbury had all told 445 H.E. bombs. In the " Baedeker " raid of June, 1942, there were 182 of those H.E. bombs and nearly 8,000 incendiaries. Clearly the Railway staff had plenty to do and to bear, and there is one point worthy of particular mention. On the suggestion of the R.T.O. the military and railway staffs underwent a course of fire drill together, and were thus able to act as a single unit in dealing with the very serious fires which Canterbury had to endure.

These are all relatively large places and I must give a word to the tragedy of one small one. This is Templecombe in Somerset, an important junction but a small village, the home of an almost entirely railway community. It looks a spot as quiet and remote from war as can be conceived, and no doubt many a westward traveller, fresh from the stress of London in the blitz, must have thought enviously how peaceful life must be there. But one day in October of 1942, the war came suddenly to Templecombe, killed thirteen people of whom five were railway men, and turned it into a village of mourning.

In a very different category, save indeed that it is to a great

extent a railway town, there is Ashford, in Kent. It was an obvious
target, not only as a junction but because of its important railway
works. Till I read its records I had several times heard people
wonder casually why Ashford had been " left alone." Why that
impression arose I do not know, but I think it did and it was wrong.
Bombs fell there for the first time as early as July, 1940, and again
in September and October, but the more severe blow came later. On
October 26th, 1942, the Heavy Machine Shops, the Brass Shop, and
the Machine Shop were all damaged, and ten men and one woman
were killed. In 1943, on March 24th, the Erecting Shop was hit.
Eight men were killed and forty-one injured, and a quarter of the shop
was temporarily lost. All things are relative, and Ashford might
have suffered more, but suffer it most unquestionably did. More
indeed might be said of it and likewise of the great marshalling yard
at Feltham, an obvious mark for enemy bombs, but as both these
places have chapters of their own I will say no more here.

Now I turn westward for three important places that suffered
grievously.

SOUTHAMPTON

If ever a place was predestined to air attack this was it. Of this
Southampton itself was perfectly aware, and made its preparations
accordingly. By the irony of fate the two first alarms were false ones.
On October 16th, 1939, a confidential message foretold an air raid,
and Mr. Biddle, the Marine Superintendent, stood by all night to
be agreeably disappointed. On May 25th, 1940, anti-aircraft fire was
heard for the first time, attacking harmlessly one of our own planes.
But there was not long to wait before the real thing, for early in
July the terminus station was hit, and a fire in the parcels office was
very pluckily put out by the staff.

That was but a curtain raiser. On the 23rd of August, bombs
were dropped in various places, and in particular on the great Inter-
national Cold Storage building at the Docks, and the flames broke out.
Within ten minutes the Docks Fire Brigade had turned out, while
bombs were still falling. The Town fire brigade came to their aid, and
so did two tugs " Neptune " and " Hector," but circumstances were
as perverse as they could be. The main water supply had had a direct

hit—this is a matter in which the Germans seem to our perhaps
jaundiced eyes to have too often had an accident to help them—and
only after some time could water be got from another source. There
was an anti-aircraft gun on the top of the building ; its ammunition
was continually exploding and fragments of shell were flying about.
So the fire still raged on the 15th, and then the wind changed, as if of
malignant purpose, and spread to the engine house. The flames had
an unctuous feast, for they consumed in all over 2,000 tons of meat,
145 tons of pork, 200 tons of odds and ends, and nearly 2,400 tons of
butter. Melted butter rode upon the waves of water and choked
the drains. On the same day the parapet at the southern end of the
store collapsed, to be followed later by the wall on the quayside.
Only on the 20th was the fire nearing its end, and by that time, to say
nothing of salt water, ten million gallons of fresh water had been
lavished upon it.

Early in September there was another false alarm ; the bells rang
through Hampshire to announce an invasion. Later in the month
there were very real raids, and real damage, but we must skip to
November. On the 15th enemy planes passed over the town, but
it was poor Coventry's turn that night. Then on the night of the
23rd/24th they came to Southampton with a vengeance. Southampton
Central Station was by no manner of means unscarred. At a first
casual glance at it in its mended state the visitor to-day may think,
marvelling, that it escaped, but it was far from doing that, and even
now there are gaps in the roof, which are the best possible evidence
to the contrary. Yet, perhaps it did escape lightly by comparison
with the main shopping centre of Southampton, which is so near it.
I have not seen either Plymouth or Coventry, but I have seen Bristol
and the City of London, and I incline to think that Southampton
presents an even greater scene of devastation. The gaping rents are
so vast that it is hard to realise that there were once shops and houses
in those desert places. If there were, then the sightseer thinks that
they were destroyed not lately but in some war of long ago, so thickly
grows the grass about the ruins.

On the night of the 23rd of November the station was ringed
with fires. Among other buildings the flames spread to the Sports
Club of the Docks and Marine Department, and in particular to the

storey on which the Club had its rifle range. Ammunition exploded in all directions, driving back the Stationmaster, Mr. Collins, and a porter who tried to tackle the flames. Even as they retired to the station they heard the whine of a bomb, flung themselves down, with pardonable impropriety, in the Ladies Waiting Room, and were buried, blinded and choked with dust and pieces of ceiling, but otherwise none the worse.

Meanwhile, great damage was being done at the Docks; the Canadian Pacific Offices were demolished, a warehouse badly damaged, and the Docks Central Fire Station with its fire engine directly hit. The *Llandovery Castle* lying at her berth also had a direct hit, and the South Western Hotel was damaged. Altogether there were 40 craters in the Old and New Docks, and though wonderfully enough no railway stock was destroyed, the track suffered at various points. All trains had to be diverted and kept away from the Southampton area, but in two days services began again.

There followed a really dreadful week-end of November 30th and December 1st, in which Southampton as a whole suffered its worst blows. The brunt of the raid of November 23rd/24th had fallen on residential districts, but now the vital business of Southampton was to be attacked and dislocated. At the Docks two warehouses were destroyed with all their stocks, and the Post Office, Harland & Wolf, and Rank's Mill were very badly damaged. The water mains were again put out of action; the only water came from the cooling plant of the electricity works, and German planes flying low were machine-gunning the fire fighters. To make things worse the weather was bitterly cold. The Stationmaster at the Central Station was surprised to see people on the line near the tunnel, and discovered some seventy soldiers in their night clothes; the house in which they had been billeted had been bombed; they had escaped just as they were and jumped over the fence on to the line in a dash for the tunnel, and stood there shivering. When that raid was over the Docks were without water, gas or electricity.

On the 5th of December the King, with Mr. Herbert Morrison and the Regional Commissioner, came to see Southampton, and before that on the 2nd the Deputy Regional Commissioner, the late Mr. Robert Bernays, had come down to help the City tackle its prob-

lems. Of these the most urgent was that of transport, and a Transport
Consultative Committee was formed with Sir William Gowers as
Chairman, on which was represented the Shipbuilding, Engineering,
and Aircraft industries, the Trades Unions, the Corporation Transport,
the Bus Company, and the Railway Company. Apart from what
may be called its normal difficulties of improving and re-arranging
their service of trains the Railway was faced with two new and
particular problems. One concerned the large amount of perishable
foodstuffs. Those who should have taken delivery of them had in
many cases lost their places of business and had not yet got new ones.
It was hard to make contact with them, and meanwhile there was an
accumulation of wagons that must be unloaded quickly. An embargo
was at once placed on the sending of more such goods to Southampton.
Then, when necessary, the Ministry of Food stepped in and made
orders for disposal. As far as possible all perishable goods that could
not be dealt with at Southampton, were moved to other stations
near by, such as Millbrook, where their owners could get at them.
One way and another, and in a remarkably short time, the owners
had re-established themselves as best they could and taken their
goods, and chaos was resolved.

The other problem was concerned with the large number of
working people who had lost their homes and had to be evacuated.
These had to be taken out of Southampton at night and brought
back to work in the morning. It was successfully done by running
special trains, and the special workmen tickets issued were for stations
as far away as Portsmouth, Winchester, Andover and Bournemouth.
There was also an increase of bus services, and by what must surely
in the circumstances have been a fine piece of organisation the evacuees
were back in Southampton every morning in time to begin their work
at 7.30. At the same time having regard to the devastation at
Southampton and the fact that the telephone was temporarily
non-existent, Train Control which had been there was moved to
Eastleigh. That is a brief, bald, dull statement, but the amount of
work it meant, and of work to be done on the instant, those only who
did it can realise. At any rate I am sure no amateur can begin to
understand it.

The railway suffered considerably from yet another raid in the early morning of June 22nd, 1941, when there came three parachute mines, two actually on the station and one very close to it ; and now, by way of relief, for the singular adventure of the unexploded bomb at Swaythling. It has a happy ending, and it shows, which is extremely soothing, that the plain man can sometimes be right and the experts all wrong. At 8.25 p.m. on January 19th, 1941, a bomb, alleged to be a 2,000 pounder, crashed through the roof of the Booking Office and through the floor. The only casualty, and a sad one, was a dog, the Leading Porter's faithful companion, lying asleep in a cupboard ; but there was a good deal of material damage, and burning coal scattered from the fireplace started a fire. The A.R.P. and the Police arrived, saw the amount of damage, declared that the bomb had exploded and that all was now over, whereupon the Booking Clerk and other members of the staff went serenely back to the Office. Next morning the landlord of the Mason's Arms over the way came in to pass the time of day, and heard that the Booking Office was occupied. Thereupon he declared that he had heard a bomb fall and that he *knew* it had not exploded. His words carried conviction, the Office was evacuated, all traffic was stopped and the Bomb Disposal people began to dig for the bomb. Not till the 6th of February was it taken away. It had *not* exploded, and if the landlord of the Mason's Arms refrained from saying " I told you so " he must be one of the most self-denying of men.

PLYMOUTH

Plymouth, as all the world knows, suffered very severely at intervals, and more particularly perhaps in March and April of 1941. It is much the same story as has been told before of other places, of hardship and danger borne by the Railway Staff with a fine courage, of damage and confusion tackled with ingenious improvisation and rapid repair. For all its inherent distinction the story might, as I am conscious, grow monotonous. But there are several interesting and original points connected with other stations which add to and vary the necessarily rather unvarying narrative, and are in one way or another intimately connected with Plymouth.

First then let us go to the little station of Turnchapel, where in November, 1940, there was fought an extraordinary and long drawn-out battle against fire. Some description of the battlefield is necessary to the understanding of it. Turnchapel is on a branch line from Plymouth Friary Station which crosses by a three span bridge an inlet of Cattewater, called Hooe Lake. There is only one platform, at the back of which is a high rocky bank. Behind this bank is a hollow in which are several Admiralty oil tanks. On the opposite side of the track is another bank a good deal lower, and beyond this is land occupied by the R.A.F. After passing through the station the line runs to a tunnel communicating with the Admiralty Depot.

On the night of November 27th a German plane dropped four bombs : two fell harmlessly in the lake, one on the bridge, and one on an oil tank behind the rocky bank. The bomb on the bridge damaged the parapet and the signal box, and buried the signalman under the ruins of a shelter, from which he was dug out unhurt. The oil tank burst instantly into flames. The fire raged all through the night, and a signalman and a porter seeing the danger to the station saved all the records at considerable risk to themselves. Next day the heat was so great that the water from the hose pipes evaporated before it could reach the flames, and deadly fumes made the work of fire fighting exceedingly dangerous. And then on the night following, that of Friday the 29th, the other tanks joined in the fray. The oil in them boiled over, and one exploded, scattering burning oil in all directions. Three A.F.S. men were killed, and the others saved themselves by jumping into the water.

The blazing oil poured in a torrent over the rocky bank and down on to the station, obliterating it on the instant. It was like a living and malign thing, a river of fire struggling and tossing to break its way out from between its banks. It flooded the track for a length of 150 yards ; it ran on to the bridge in one direction, and as far as the tunnel in the other. It climbed and crossed the lower bank on the further side of the track and so invaded the R.A.F., but luckily did no harm there. Next it fell on to the road leading to the station, flooded that and flowed on into the other river—of water. The channel is here 100 feet wide, but the oil took that in its fiery stride and set alight to a timber yard on the far side. Some of the blazing timber was thrown into the water and the rest was moved and saved.

It was not till the night of Sunday, December 1st, that the fire was at last put out. The station buildings had vanished; lamp standards and automatic machines survived as cripples, furiously twisted by the flames; the rails of the track were bent into fantastic shapes and the signal box which had partially withstood the bomb was now utterly destroyed. Yet in under a fortnight there was a temporary signal box and a newly laid track and freight trains were running; by the 16th passenger service was again normal.

Another station which came into prominence through the Plymouth raids, though in a much less calamitous way, was Bere Alston, which lies across the water from Plymouth. It only came in for the tail end of the raids, and, incidentally, a curve in the line there saved a fully loaded passenger train; it was being pursued along the line by a German airman, who luckily did not see the curve, and so dropped his bombs wide. Bere Alston became at times the only conduit pipe for information between Plymouth and Exeter, so that the Station Master was once on duty continuously for three days and nights. But the most marked effect that the raids had on it was a large and sudden increase of passenger traffic. Every evening as blackout approached people poured out of Plymouth to avoid nights of bombing, and went back to work next morning. Many of them had lost their homes and all they possessed. Ultimately they found room in billets or in barns or village halls, but before these could be organised they spent the nights wherever they could, often wandering about the country lanes till daybreak. I remember to have seen something of a similar exodus from Bath, where I chanced, greatly to my own discomfort, to be during the two nights of the " Baedeker " raid in 1942. On the second night people were climbing up the hill to Sham Castle to spend the night as best they could in a bitter April wind; and a stream of refugees is a horrid and disquieting sight, if one is not used to it, though it has become common enough in Europe. These fugitives of Bere Alston became for some while regular passengers like those of the Chislehurst Caves on a smaller scale. Witness these statistics; for the week ending April 22nd, 259 tickets were issued from the station; for that ending May 19th, the number was 1,041.

The third station to have greatness thrust upon it by the Plymouth raids was Wadebridge, far away in North Cornwall, a name which

ay primarily suggest to many people, as it does to me, the noble
nks of St. Enodoc. Never before in railway history had that most
ordly of Great Western trains, the Cornish Riviera express, so far
emeaned itself as to pass through comparatively humble Wadebridge.
This was due to the mutual arrangement for exchange of lines between
he two Companies, and Plymouth was at the bottom of it. The
Great Western main line traffic both to and from Cornwall travelled
on the Southern's Cornwall line in order to avoid Plymouth. The
rains from Penzance and Truro travelled by Bodmin Road, joined
he Southern at Boscarne Junction, went on to Wadebridge and
Okehampton, and rejoined the Great Western at Exeter St. Davids.
Nor was it merely a question of making what Tony Lumpkin called
" circumbendibus." Owing to a steep gradient at Delabole,
assenger trains from the North Cornwall line were limited to eight
oaches and freight trains to 29 vehicles. There is moreover a
urther regulation that a 20-ton van must be at the rear of the train.
o when a Great Western train arrived, as it might do, with too
many coaches, or with a 20-ton van in front and 16-ton van behind,
here was something in the nature of a jig-saw puzzle, with a breaking
p or re-arranging of trains, and consequently with inevitably long
waits at Wadebridge. However, this ill wind blew somebody good,
or the passengers often spent the time of waiting in forays on the
own for food. This emergency plan was in force from April 23rd
o 26th, and then again from April 29th till May 2nd as regards
assenger traffic, and three days longer for goods traffic. It involved
great deal of hard work and long hours, as may be imagined, and
ne man at least must have been glad when it ended; the Station
Foreman at Wadebridge was hard at it for seventeen hours at a stretch.
And this is only one illustration of the way in which the Southern and
he Great Western helped each other in their difficulties. As just
ne more example, April 23rd, 1941, saw all communication between
Plymouth and Devonport cut off and an emergency service had to be
rranged with Exeter, the Great Western trains running over the
outhern lines. Five days later by way of tit-for-tat Southern trains
ravelled over the Great Western lines from Exeter, while G.W.R.
rains were still using the S.R. North Cornwall lines. In short each
ine came to the rescue of the other with unfailing readiness.

PORTSMOUTH

As early as June, 1940, Portsmouth became a target for enemy attack; by August there had been a series of daylight raids; as the months went on night raids became heavy and constant, and may be said to have culminated towards the end of April when thirty land-mines were dropped in one night. The station at Portsmouth Harbour probably suffered devastation at least as severe as any other on the whole Southern system, and Portsmouth itself, Fratton and Gosport all had their full share. As ever, the railwaymen rose admirably to the occasion, and nowhere perhaps had they more to bear in regard to their personal losses in houses and property. There was such ruin that they devised their own system for giving immediate help in the cases in which it was most sorely needed. A fund was started to which over seven hundred members paid a contribution of sixpence a week. Up to April, 1941, more than £550 had been raised, but the damage was too great, the fund became almost insolvent, and an appeal for voluntary contributions was made to many stations on the Southern system, and was generously responded to; a good example of comradeship on the part of those who had plenty of trouble of their own but sympathised with those of others that were still greater.

It was on August 12th that a bomb fell at the Harbour Station on the pier end of the concourse, set light to buildings, offices and the pier itself, gutted the access to the landing stage, smashed the water main, damaged four trains, closed the station and caused a number of casualties including one man killed.

This is the old story which I have had to tell often before subject to variations, but on the 26th of August comes one of an unexploded bomb which is a little different. It is interesting as showing the kind of problem that had no doubt often to be solved the risks that had to be estimated and run in order that vital traffic should get through, and the fine courage with which volunteers were ready to face dangers outside the ordinary run of those endured every day. The story can be told in the series of messages that reached the Southern Railway Headquarters at Deepdene, and the answers that were given.

At 6.30 p.m. on August 26th the news reached Deepdene that an unexploded bomb had been found just over the railway boundary close to the Green Lane Signal Box at Fratton, and that all traffic was being stopped at Cosham and Havant and turned back. At 8.15 came another message that the Bomb Disposal Officer thought that it would be safe to have a single line working on the Down Line, if a protective screen of thirty empty box wagons was placed on the Up Line. Two and a half hours later this opinion was backed up by the Area Defence Officer from Portsmouth. The Railway Company replied that they were not prepared to take the risk, and could not allow traffic to pass, on the grounds, first that if the bomb exploded the screen of box wagons might be smashed and parts of them be hurled against the passing train, second, that even if no train were passing the permanent way might be littered and damaged by the debris of the box wagons, third, that the safety of the train crew must be considered. Ten minutes later came the Ministry of Transport urging that there was important traffic on the way to the Dockyard ; but the Railway Company stood firm that the danger to the men was too great.

That was that for the night. Next morning came the news that the bomb was of a kind that could not be handled for two or three days, and the consequent suggestion from the Ministry that high-sided wagons should be employed as a screen, while the men should be ordered to lie down on their stomachs as they passed the danger point. Thereupon after further consultation the Traffic Manager decided not to order any man to take the risk, but to call for volunteers. There was an instant and splendid response. The Traffic and Locomotive Running staff at Portsmouth and Fratton volunteered almost to a man, and the crews of the down trains, not to be outdone in gallantry, entirely refused to be relieved by the volunteers sent to meet them at the edge of the danger zone. As a result twenty-four freight trains of great importance had passed through the zone four days after the bomb had fallen. The Railway Executive Committee said that it was " a fine performance "—three words of praise, but they came from those who were railwaymen. Nobody else can, or need, embroider them.

To return to what may be called the ordinary routine, there was serious damage at Fratton and at Portsmouth Harbour on December 5th, and then, passing over minor incidents, since bombs like other things are relative, came one of Portsmouth's real nights, that of January 10/11th, 1941, when all traffic was stopped and both high explosive and incendiary bombs fell at Portsmouth and Southsea Portsmouth Harbour, Fratton and Gosport. The girders supporting the Harbour Station were at one point blown away so that one coach of a train crashed down on to the mud below. There were fires everywhere, the water main was hit, the tide was right out so that no water could be got from below the station. The saving of the station was clearly beyond hope, and all that could be done was to save as many movables as possible.

The tenth day of the month was an unlucky one for Portsmouth for, on March 10th, bombs came down from 8.0 p.m. to 2.0 a.m. without surceàse. April 8th, April 10th, and April 17th were all bad nights, and then came the 27th with its thirty land-mines Portsmouth and Southsea Station had two of them, and there was much damage and several fatal casualties. As a small incident, racks of tickets were blown down and tickets scattered everywhere among the debris. If this brought anyone hope of free travel, that hope was disappointed for the tickets were all most carefully retrieved under the travelling auditor's eye and withdrawn from stock.

The raids did not cease with April for May 3rd/4th was a very bad night, when a staff air raid shelter on the Dock at Portsmouth and Southsea had a direct hit (mercifully several of the staff had just left it) and a delayed action bomb added greatly to the difficulties. The people in the Isle of Wight who read their Sunday papers that morning little knew that they owed them to three intrepid volunteers, a driver, a fireman and a guard, who passed within ten feet of the bomb to get the papers to the boat. As soon as possible the bomb disposal squad tackled the bomb but it ticked ominously and they had to leave it to explode, which it accordingly did, and added its quota to the damage.

This service of boats to and from the Isle of Wight was, by the way, far from being without its dangers and there was one serious disaster in the early morning of September 20th, 1941. The *Portsdown* struck a mine and was lost, together with eight out of her crew of eleven, and some twelve passengers. Here is the description of the look-out man, Jupe by name :—

"We left Portsmouth Harbour Pier at 4.0 a.m. and I took up my position as look-out in the bows of the *Portsdown*. After we had cleared the harbour Channel buoys I reported this to Captain Chandler on the bridge and the vessel was then rounded up to go through the swashway to continue our journey to Ryde. About a minute after this, and before the vessel had completed her alteration of course, I heard a sort of scraping noise alongside the port side of the ship, and then, after what must have been a few seconds, there was a terrific explosion. At this moment I was looking out across the port bow and I was thrown into the sea. When I came to the surface I grasped a piece of floating wood and swam to the after port side sponson, when I climbed on board and assisted in getting out the lifeboats, both of which were lowered and loaded with passengers."

As soon as possible after the explosion a naval pinnace went out and saved seventeen people.

DAMAGE AND DELAY THROUGH ENEMY ACTION
INCIDENTS PER 100 ROUTE MILES

	Route Mileage	Number of incidents	Incidents per 100 Route Miles
SOUTHERN RAILWAY	2,135	3,637	170
G.W.R.	3,652	1,202	33
L.M.S.	6,672	1,939	29
L.N.E.R.	6,278	1,737	28

First recorded incident on the Southern Railway, June 19th, 1940
Last recorded incident on the Southern Railway, March 23rd, 1945

Chapter V

D-DAY—BEFORE AND AFTER

WITH the earliest days of Spring in 1944 began the long
tension of waiting for the invasion of Europe. May
came and surely now must be the appointed time, but
day followed day till the month was spent and nothing had happened.
In a story of Rudyard Kipling's there is a description of how in a
sinking ship the water level pauses before it falls with a crash upon
the deck ; " it looked like a silver wire laid down along the bulwarks
and I thought it was never going to break." So it was now with
the line of ships drawn along our southern coast. Then with the
6th of June the crash came and for a moment the taut line snapped,
but there succeeded a new tension almost as intolerable and even
longer drawn out.

Even so in writing I have seen D-Day looming ahead of me
complex and formidable, and now it has arrived and must be tackled.
At the very start it must be said that D-Day was only one incident,
though a tremendous one. It is like the topmost peak in a great
range of mountains stretching out both before and beyond it. The
full tide of invasion was at Southampton on that particular and fateful
day, but it had been rising for a long time and it went on thundering
along our coast for many a day afterwards. That one day and that
one place form only part of the story of the gigantic movement
technically known as Operation " O " or " Overlord." Dynamo
had been the code word for the rescue of the British Army from

Building parts for " Mulberry " in the King George V Graving Dock at Southampton

Dunkirk and Overlord was the secret name for the converse and infinitely greater movement of two armies, British and American, back to France after four years, for the liberation of Europe. Before D-Day came the process of the " build-up" and after it that of the " follow-up." With the actual day of invasion the rush of ships and men and stores did not slacken in the smallest degree. It changed in character when once the first adventure had been successfully undertaken and a bridgehead had been established, but it was no less strenuous. It had taken some two years to prepare for D-Day and from D-Day to V.E. Day the rush went on, sinking a little at intervals and then rising again to a fresh crest of endeavour.

If in those spring days of 1944 some observer from another planet had been perched high in the air with a bird's eye view of the south and south-west of England, it would soon have occurred to him that something vast and strange and, as far as could be, secret was going on. He would have seen troops and stores on the move, occasionally by road but chiefly by train. First of all he would have noticed them in small streams and then in great rivers, gradually converging in one direction. The biggest streams of all would have been pouring towards the Docks at Southampton, but there would have been numberless minor ones flowing to all the ports from Tilbury to Falmouth. If that observer could have peeped through the leaves of the trees in the New Forest he would have seen the stores steadily accumulating there, carried by what has been called the tarpaulin armada. He would have noticed that the trees of the Forest had been cut away by the side of the railway line and that sidings full of wagons had taken their places. New sidings were growing up almost overnight like mushrooms. At various places along the coast too, he would have seen strange craft assembled, the L.C.A.'s (landing craft assault) and L.S.T.'s (landing ship tanks), with bows that opened and came down to form a ramp to a quay or a beach.

One spot, which would have particularly whetted his curiosity, was Lockerley, buried in its woods and yet only a few miles from Southampton. I must pause for a moment to describe it. Very few people have ever heard of Lockerley and if the Germans had, they made no use of their knowledge. Yet it was the great storehouse of the American Army against D-Day. There were its tanks and guns and ammunition. There were fifteen miles of sidings and a hundred and thirty-four big covered sheds stretching for three miles among the concealing trees. There can be few quieter stations under the sun than Dunbridge and yet it handled all the Lockerley traffic. When I went to look for it down a narrow by-road after passing through Romsey, we found a tiny station dreaming in the hot sunlight, wholly deserted, the signal box empty, the day's trains clearly gone. Surely this must be the end of our quest but no, this was Mottisfont and we must wander on a little further between the hedgerows. We found it at last, equally trim and quiet, almost equally small, having only oil lamps and getting its water from the public house, equally deserted save by the kind Station Master who awaited us. There was something magical about it as about the figures the Station Master gave us. In June, 1938, by way of comparison Dunbridge had dealt with 182 wagons. In June, 1944, it dealt with 5,246 (to say nothing of 6,117 parcels) and in the whole of that year with 33,000. The building of Lockerley began in October, 1943, and here in months and wagons is the story of its rise to the peak of D-Day and of its subsequent decline : January 898, February 1,156, March 2,588, April 2,847, May 3,476, June 5,246, July 4,359, August 2,604, September 1,761. By September Lockerley and Dunbridge had done the greater part of their great work and soon the little station could return to dreaming, full of glorious memories, and in the intervals devote itself to the strawberry traffic.

Yes, Lockerley would unquestionably have told our observer that something great and mysterious was on foot, but perhaps even more puzzling and exciting would have seemed certain vast monsters in Southampton Docks. Months before, in October of 1943, 500 men working night and day in a dry dock had begun building concrete caissons, each of them 200 feet long, 56 feet wide and 60 feet high. As they were finished the dry dock was flooded and the monsters, still in embryo, floated away to wet berths near by to be completed. At the same time in the King George V Graving Dock were being built from pre-fabricated parts the " Rhino " pontoons—six rows of thirty tanks each, for ferrying tanks and armoured vehicles. There were other curious objects too, " spuds " by name, great vertical columns, which should anchor to the sea bed the " whales," pier heads built elsewhere and then towed to Southampton. Concrete monoliths rearing their heads forty feet out of the sea were being floated down Portsmouth Harbour and disappearing for some unknown destination. It was as if the giants of Stonehenge had taken to the water. All these mysterious things were components of the now famous port called "Mulberry." How much those knew who helped to make them I do not know. Perhaps a good many people knew just a very little but only a few knew all or anything like all. The vertical columns were very generally believed to be the supporters of colossal nets in which submarines were to be trapped, and to my hypothetical observer in the sky those ponderous forms would have been beyond all comprehension; but they would have heightened his impression that something was going to happen on an unexampled scale. And in trying now to look back nearly all of us were in a like case with him. We felt rather than knew that an immense co-ordinated movement such as had never been attempted before was steadily taking shape, but of that shape we knew next to nothing. The secret as a whole remained wonderfully well kept.

Let us try to see something of what those in the secret had to do for many months beforehand in the way of planning. We must bear in mind (I have said this before of other movements but it cannot be rubbed in too hard or too often) that the workaday world did not stand still to oblige them; the railway had all the while to cope with its normal and very heavy traffic and with other movements for Government not connected with D-Day. In the embarking of the original B.E.F. and of the expedition to North Africa—great tasks but drops in the ocean as compared with this one—only the British Army had been involved. Now there were two armies and perfect co-ordination with the Americans had to be ensured. The one essential point in the preliminary planning was to decide on the greatest amount of tonnage that could be dealt with at each port area and which depot, British or American, should be served by each port. The force served by a port announced its needs and it was for the Freights Movement Directorate at the War Office to consider these various bids for tonnage. Skeleton time tables were made up between every depot and every port, and these were gradually filled in with times of arrival and departure, and the code number of each train, by which it could be summoned on the instant, the maximum number of its wagons and the path, sometimes a tortuous one, it was to follow. There was a system of priorities for goods traffic ranging from No. 1 priority for operational purposes at the top to non-essential civilian traffic at the bottom. There was a daily conference at 10 o'clock every morning between the War Office and Headquarters at Deepdene. Since all the railway companies worked together, there was every morning the Inter-Company Operating Conference made possible by a special telephone circuit linking up the Chief Operating Officers of each of the four companies. Constant touch was maintained with the United States Transportation Officers.

From its geographical position the heaviest burden again fell on the Southern, and the new traffic problems involved the building of many new sidings. We may first look at this problem from a Southampton point of view. First came the long inflow of traffic. As early as December, 1943, Longparish, by way of example, was doing a fine trade in bombs, in particular " block busters." In that month it received 478 wagons of bombs and by April in 1944 the number had risen to 1,451. Petrol was pouring in a steady stream into many places in Hampshire and Dorset. Gradually this flood of petrol rose and rose till the end of April and then its outflow to Southampton and the other ports began. Petrol is only one thing among so many but a mightily important one, and here a word must be said about one more well-kept secret, the system of pipe lines which conveyed oil across England from west to east.

As far as the Southern Railway was concerned it was twofold. There was first the construction of 72 miles of pipe line from Walton-on-Thames to the ultimate destination near Lydd. It had to be done quickly and between the 12th of June, 1943, and the end of July materials had been conveyed to the spot, representing nearly 8,000 tons of pipes, each approximately 40 feet long, weighing eight and a half hundredweights and having a diameter of eight inches. There were another 459 tons of pipes, some of them lighter, to be taken to Appledore and Lydd. The 72 miles were divided into six sections, each under a separate contractor and engineer, and the sections were served by different railheads. There was secondly the making of 26 miles of pipe line from Paddock Wood to Port Victoria, for which the materials were all despatched in less than a month between July and August, 1943, and this meant another 1,357 tons of pipes from 35 to 50 feet long and eighteen inches in diameter. Motor lorries tractors and cranes all played their part and the line was ready in good time.

To return to the traffic of the build-up, it is not difficult to imagine what puzzles arose at small stations where Government dumps were created or which became railheads for dumps or aerodromes. The Government traffic at times held up that of ordinary trade, and even so it was cramped for space. At Brockenhurst, Christchurch, Lyndhurst Road and Beaulieu the difficulties were often acute. The traffic in tanks and vehicles at Andover Junction was enormous and the Station Master at Winchester declared that he never wanted to hear the name of a tank again. To relieve the situation new marshalling yards came into being at Micheldever and Brockenhurst and there was already Eastleigh. Eastleigh, Micheldever and Feltham together could not cope with the Southampton traffic ; so Brockenhurst, with its seven new sidings hewn out of the forest, came to the rescue and helped to sort it out. In case of bombs it was as well to have as many baskets as possible for vital eggs. Micheldever and Brockenhurst between them relieved the pressure on Eastleigh. To one of the two all the down goods traffic normally dealt with in the East Yard at Eastleigh was handed over ; that left sixteen Eastleigh Sidings for the " Overlord " traffic and another eight near by were also earmarked to be used later for the purpose.

Micheldever is one of the places which have had railway fame thrust upon them by the war. Its name was familiar enough, and so was a doubt as to how to pronounce it, to any one who travelled on the line to Southampton in peace time, but it had then looked placid enough. In 1937 when the present Station Master first came there it had no marshalling yard and had one down goods and one up goods train a day. With the war came seventeen marshalling sidings with a shunting staff working twenty four hours a day, seven days a week, and during the " Overlord " rush it was turning over a thousand wagons a day. The increase in the outward down traffic was largely due to the placing there of the Ordnance Emergency Depot. It was called by an irreverent but well deserved compliment the Woolworth depot, for it provided everything in the world except clothing, from a nut to the engine for a tank.

At this depot was a staff of between one and two thousand soldiers and a shed over 2,000 feet long, with overhead electric cranes. Anything urgently wanted in France was indented for (I hope I have still enough of the Ordnance language) direct on Micheldever. When I could talk that language fluently there used to be unpleasant messages called " hasteners " but apparently none were ever wanted at Micheldever, for if the indent came in one afternoon, the stores were sent off next morning by a 4.0 a.m. train and a special vessel laden with " Priority No. 1 " material for France.

This talk of supplies to France has carried me prematurely ahead, and I must retrace my steps to the build-up and go further west than Southampton. The same processes, if not on so big a scale, were going on there, too. Before D-Day there had been accumulated 35,000 tons of stores and ammunition, mostly for the American Army, at Launceston, Tower Hill, Whitstone and Halwill. All that mass had arrived from America at ports in South Wales and South Cornwall for despatch to France from Plymouth. A month or so after D-Day only 4,000 tons of it remained in all the country-side. Here, too, were new sidings at Lydford, which became an auxiliary yard to Plymouth. And in this matter the West Country must surely hold the speed record for its achievement at the American Naval Depot at Newcourt. It was at 12.10 p.m.—let me be exact—on Saturday, October 2nd, 1943, that the Western Divisional Superintendent was asked by the American Naval Authorities to meet them at 2.30 that day to discuss the making of a temporary siding beside the line between Topsham and Exmouth Junction, in order that 150 wagons of stores then on their way from the North might be unloaded. The land on which the siding was wanted was then a green field. He went to the meeting with the Divisional Engineer, who undertook to have the material to lay 1,200 feet of siding on the spot by 11.0 a.m. on Monday the 4th. He was within an hour of keeping his word, for it was there by noon. By noon on the Tuesday American personnel had 1,000 feet of siding on the ground and the Divisional Engineer's staff had the running line connection laid in and had made the shallow embankment to carry the turn-out to the siding. Early

on Wednesday morning the turn-out was joined up to the siding, and
by noon wagons were in position. The Signal and Telegraph Department had not been idle, having put up new telegraph poles and
shifted wires. By five o'clock on that Wednesday afternoon the
siding complete with signalling was in use.

I have put the stores first because they take longer to move, and
so the moving of them begins earlier. Now for the men to use
them. There were earlier moves of the troops from training grounds
to depots, but here we are concerned with those for D-Day, and
these were in two parts. There was first the accumulation of men in
their concentration areas, mainly in the south and south-west; second,
the move into marshalling areas for their respective ports, with
Southampton as the chief point of embarkation, many of the ports
being supplemented by " hards," from which men and vehicles could
embark in landing craft. March 26th was the appointed day for the
beginning of the first movement, June 3rd, for that of the second,
which was steadily intensified until the 9th. I have tried hitherto to
separate the periods before and after D-Day, but here it is impossible,
for the operation was quite continuous. After the 9th there came a
short and only comparative lull, because the casualties had been
smaller than expected, and so the flow of men instantly needed was
smaller, too. The full pressure began again on the 12th, and from
that day till the 22nd was at its heaviest. From the 23rd to 26th
the storm in the Channel brought movements almost to a full-stop,
and then came another rush. Till the middle of September there
was no slightest surcease and after that the flow of troops settled down
to a lesser but steady pace, with one or two minor " peaks," and so
went on till V.E. Day. Train after train during all those months
moved to its appointed port, watched on its road by ever vigilant
control officers, with no man on board knowing what that port was,
the only legend on the warrants being " To unknown destination."

The same conferences, the same schedules and time-tables, the
same minute plans, and sometimes the same sudden change of plans
were needed for the men, as I have tried to describe before for the
stores, and I will not repeat them. As far as was humanly possible,
all these preparations had been plotted long beforehand, but there
was another movement of personnel that had to be made at the

shortest notice and on the top of all the rest. D-Day was scarcely passed when there came the flying bombs. This meant re-distribution of the Anti-Aircraft and Balloon units from all over the country, and without a moment to spare. As our soldiers overran the bomb sites in France there came a rest for the south of England, but none for Kent, Essex, Suffolk, and Norfolk, and none for the railways. Once again, and in a very few days, guns and balloons must be moved to defend the new areas attacked. And all the while operation " Overlord " must go on uninterrupted. Gradually, moreover, as the victorious easterly surge in France went on, there came more competing or rather supplementary traffic at home—men coming home on leave, prisoners of war, the ever-mounting mass of mails for two Armies ; but these belong definitely to the times after D-Day, and will fall into their places later. So back to the days before the day.

" It does not take a long time," said Madame Defarge to her husband, " for an earthquake to swallow a town. But when it is ready, it takes place and grinds to pieces everything before it. In the meantime it is always preparing, though it is not seen or heard. That is your consolation." That was everybody's consolation, but everybody wanted to know when. There were one or two clues, though they were vague ones. Just over two months before D-Day there was imposed a coastal ban covering the coast line from the Wash to Land's End and, roughly speaking, ten miles inland. There was the cancelling of certain passenger trains, even old familiar friends by which people had travelled for years. Great care was taken in telling the press of such cancellations. Only small bits of information were let out at a time. People were told of the trains they could catch rather than of those they could not. But under the heavy pressure of " Overlord " traffic the trains did disappear. Electric trains showed a 30 per cent. decrease as compared with the winter traffic of pre-war days, and during non-business hours the mileage was actually down by 60 per cent. To railway workers at any rate, there was a third clue, in a stirring message from the General Manager, with a fine touch of Napoleon before Waterloo, " To all Southern Railway men and women. The hour of greatest effort and action is approaching." That was issued on the 19th of May, and eighteen days later the hour had come.

The railways were the conduit pipes to the ports; so now for he ports, and first of all Southampton Docks. After 1940 there ad been a lull there until lease-lend began to function. Then from early in 1942 the Docks were busy once more. The first sight of the Docks is normally to the stranger as that of a mighty forest of cranes and there were more cranes wanted. There is a network of railway sidings and there were more sidings wanted, too. There was a plan o be made, a secret berthing plan known by the letter K, showing where every type of vessel could be placed with the greatest economy of space, and it had to be revised again and again. The statistics of what was done at Southampton are overwhelming and some of them are set out in the appendices; but I cannot resist a few. This, for instance, as to the stores : the military tonnage dealt with in the seventeen weeks after D-Day equalled the combined exports and imports of the whole fifty-two weeks of the year 1938. Or this as to the men : the figures of personnel embarked and disembarked from D-Day to V.E. Day are, British 364,350, U.S. Army 2,165,883. Add to this a little matter of 310,113 prisoners of war, and the total s 2,840,346 men.

The layman's imagination is stunned at the thought of just a few of the problems that arose, and there are many more of which he has never thought at all. The fact that there were at times 3,000 wagons inside the Docks may faintly suggest the difficulties of that perpetually silting traffic. Those in authority had provided for fifty per cent. being lost in the landing. The estimate was mercifully falsified, replacements were not necessary on such a scale, and this inevitably had its reactions both on shipping and on railways. There was the recurring problem of keeping the Docks clear of empty wagons and a special body was set up to review this one question. Again the exact sequence of trains into the Docks and the way in which the stores had been packed in them was incalculably important. Heavy tanks must be loaded in the bottom of the ship's hold, and lighter cargo on the top; but suppose the train of lighter stores arrived before the tanks, there must be a hold-up when every minute was valuable. As far as possible plans were made three days ahead, and once the next day's train had started on its way from the forwarding point it could not be stopped. These are a few samples given

in the hope that they may make the reader's head spin as they do mine
And here is one little fact which may appease that reader's innocent
curiosity, also as it does mine. When did those on the spot know the
day on which all this terrific accumulation of men and stores was to
take final shape and all that arduous planning to give its proofs?
Well, here is one answer. The Divisional Officer at Southampton
knew on Tuesday, May 30th, that is to say, six days before the
originally appointed D-Day, the Fifth of June.

We will leave Southampton to return to it at the supreme moment
and take a glance—no more—at some of the other Southern Railway
ports reinforcing it. First Poole and Hamworthy close to it. Both
were concerned with the petrol traffic; Poole for the U.S.A. and
Hamworthy for Britain. When the Americans decided to load petrol
to ships at Poole, the yard had to be cleared of all other traffic, the
sidings must be realigned and cartage plant increased. Petrol is
" kittle " stuff and the greatest care had to be taken; the train in
charge of dispatch riders and a military guard, was propelled and not
hauled along the single line to the quay, while patrols rigorously
stopped all smoking. In the middle of May petrol began to arrive.
700 tons of it on one day, and the really intense traffic set in on the
3rd of June—over 3,500 tons by the end of the month, followed by
over 8,000 in July. Hamworthy fed the British forces with petrol,
flame-throwing and Diesel oil. It came to its peak a little later than
Poole, for the full tide of its traffic did not begin to flow till ten days
after D-Day. Then it made up for lost time and up to the end of
July the port had handled 20,000 tons of oil.

Lymington in the Solent had its slipways doubled so that two
tank landing craft could load simultaneously. On the Saturday before
D-Day L.C.I.'s were being loaded with troops there. And so on to
Portsmouth, where as early as the beginning of May two ships, the
Shanklin and the *Merstone*, had been practising the carrying of troops,
their crews cut off from the outer world, as long as their exercises
lasted, and forbidden to communicate with the shore. At the end
of May the *Shanklin* was carrying Naval officers and men to their
ships at Spithead. On the 3rd she and the *Merstone* began to make
trips to ships in the Solent, this time with soldiers. As D-Day drew
nearer the Solent was solid with shipping, and someone with pardon-

able exaggeration said it was possible to walk from Portsmouth to Southampton by stepping from ship to ship.

Further east again Littlehampton was busy with ammunition. Early in May nine barges had come into the river, taken on board some 2,700 tons of ammunition, and then remained waiting for the day. Later there came nine ships also full of ammunition, their task to follow up quickly after the first landing. Later again a ship a day left Littlehampton, and by the end of August some 18,000 tons of ammunition had been sent from this one port alone. So along the coast to Newhaven, which had been closed to all normal commercial traffic in July, 1940, though reopened a year later for coastwise traffic in coal. Newhaven had received some of the men from Dunkirk, and now it was sending them the other way. As the time drew near the harbour was almost choked with small craft, and from D-Day itself to ten days after it there was a continuous flow of troops. By the end of June, 62,000 men had sailed from Newhaven, and by the end of July, 100,000 more.

And now the great moment has almost come. Southampton at least must have had a good guess, for on the Saturday, June 3rd, Mr. Churchill had been there to see for himself, and the Minister of War Transport on the Sunday. To stand at the furthest point of the Docks jutting into the water and then to look back is to gain an impression of almost inconceivable bigness, with Southampton itself in the remote distance. As one gazes to-day at that great stretch one has to try to see it in imagination as it was on the eve of D-Day, with innumerable landing craft assembled at their berths, packed six and seven and eight deep. They would soon be bruised and battered, but now they were bright and new, so that one who beheld them declared that he must be looking at a colossal regatta. There was one thought that must have been in everybody's mind— what a target for the bombers ! They must come or try to come and there was every preparation to welcome them, but they never did.

The 5th of June passed ; General Eisenhower took the brave and tremendous responsibility of decision, and on the 6th the Armada slipped away for Normandy. All the way there was a great lane of ships. Every few minutes flights of our bombers went over, and the reassuring voices of the spotters sang out " Friendly planes overhead." With this sea adventure operation " Neptune," there come back to us names which had so stirring a sound in the story of that other adventure of Dunkirk. Here, once more, were the Southern Railway boats—*Canterbury*, *Biarritz*, *Isle of Guernsey*, *Maid of Orleans*, *Dinard*, The first four were L.S.I. (landing ship infantry), and *Dinard*, a hospital carrier. They had been earmarked for their tasks long beforehand, and had taken part in so many exercises that the men grew weary of them, always hoping that the real thing was coming and always disappointed. They had been to the Clyde, to Scapa, and to the Firth of Forth. They had been used as targets for dive-bombing practice. The *Maid of Orleans* had carried Mr. Churchill and the Naval and Military staffs from Gareloch to the *Queen Mary*, on the way to the Quebec Conference, and taken many troops to Inverary for intensive training. The *Canterbury* had been wholly transformed from her ancient state of the *Golden Arrow* days. Her four lounges had been stripped and filled with hammocks for troops ; cabins and alcoves along her sides had been ripped out to make room for supports for landing craft davits ; her deck had been strengthened and covered with some substance in the nature of concrete. Now the respective captains had been briefed for D-Day, and the men had an inkling that this last " big exercise " was something more.

There could not be any prelude to the story of these ships half so good as the speech of Captain Payne of the *Maid of Orleans* to all hands mustered in the saloon in Cowes Roads. By great good luck I have got a copy of it—not from Captain Payne himself—and whether he likes it or not it shall be set down. It is at once so inspiring and so homely, so practical and so perfectly attuned to its audience that I would no more dare to paraphrase a word of it than I would the speech of Henry V before the feast of Crispian.

" Well, lads, I am not telling you what to do because I know you will do it. The time has come when we are called upon to help in the great effort of liberating Europe, and you men of the Merchant Service do not require a lot of detailed instructions. Given the bare outline of a job, you do it without the blare of trumpets, but by sheer indomitable guts, exactly the same as those old-timers who beat the sailing ships round the Horn. The Empire is watching and will be proud of you; the Company will be proud of you, and I am sure will remember each one of you as their men who sailed in one of their ships on that glorious day. I know you all personally, and I promise that in the days to come I will do my utmost to help you and remind the authorities that you were of the gallant group who sailed on that eventful evening with a light heart and firm resolve. By doing your duty quietly you will be helping me and by so doing helping each other. Our job is to deliver the troops and keep on delivering. My job is triple, the safe conduct of the troops and you, but that doesn't worry me, because I know you will help me. An appropriate omen— Joan of Arc, Maid of Orleans, liberated France; this *Maid* will help to do so again by the grace of God. Do not think I am any braver than you because I am not. I would much rather be in my garden at peace or in a pub, but this job has got to be done or you and yours would become worse than slaves. And when this show is over you will be able to walk with dignity among your friends both in Britain and France. Good luck to you all."

Let us follow the *Maid* on her voyage. By just after two o'clock on the morning of the 6th she reached the swept Channel. At 5.40 she anchored at the lowering position. In five minutes the L.C.A.'s (landing craft assault) were manned, and at five minutes past six they were lowered. Three-quarters of an hour later the L.C.I.'s (landing craft infantry) arrived alongside, but the L.C.M.'s (landing craft motors) were late, since the weather had been too bad for them to make the crossing up to time. There was great difficulty in making our L.C.'s fast alongside, owing to the heavy swell running, and some damage was done both to the landing craft and to the *Maid* herself, which was holed in the starboard quarters below the main deck level. Between 9.50 and 10.30 five of the L.C.A.'s returned and were hoisted aboard, and during all that time the ship had to be manœuvred to give them a lee, while oil was poured to windward to lessen the breaking waves. While the ship was at anchor and later after the convoy of which she was one had been ordered to proceed, she came under heavy gunfire from enemy shore batteries, and all the ships were ordered to make smoke until they were out of range.

The *Maid* made many more trips, but on June 28th she made her last. On this day Captain Payne could not be there, and she was commanded by Captain Masters. Some of those on board of her had had no sleep for three nights. She had just landed 800 troops on the beaches, and was coming up Channel for home when she struck a mine, and there was a violent explosion. There was a big hole in her starboard side, all the lights went out, and the ship was enveloped in a cloud of smoke and steam. " The old girl is going," said Captain Masters ; four lifeboats and one L.C.A. were got away, and all left the ship except the Captain and four other officers. Then, when it was clear that no one else was left alive on board, they threw three rafts into the sea and jumped for it. From the rafts they boarded an L.C.A. and ultimately a destroyer. In half an hour from the time she was struck the poor *Maid* sank stern first. One engineer and three firemen had been instantaneously killed by the explosion, and the third engineer, J. L. Crockart, D.S.O., before named for his bravery at Dunkirk, was so badly injured that he died in hospital.

The hospital carrier *Dinard* also struck a mine, but was luckier than the poor *Maid*, for she lived to do good service again. It was on D+1-Day on her way to Juno beach that she struck the mine, and she was making water and sent out distress calls. Two minesweepers were near at hand and took off all but those necessary to the ship's safety. Within half an hour a tug appeared and towed the *Dinard* to the beachhead where she stayed for the night. The bulkheads were shored up and the next night, after an anxious voyage in a fresh sea, with her forepart nearly falling off, she anchored in St. Helens Roads. On the 9th she was towed into Southampton and went into dry dock whence she emerged by the middle of July, patched up and fit to carry on.

The *Canterbury*, like the *Maid*, made her first trip on June 6th, and reached the mine-swept Channel just as dawn was breaking ; and the land loomed dimly ahead. Everything went like clockwork, though the weather was as rough as any encountered in the exercises. The landing craft all got away successfully and Captain Walker says he felt sorry for the men who were sure to be sea sick before they reached the shore—a little touch that adds to our composite picture of the whole enterprise. He was likewise a little sorry for himself for an odd reason; the possibilities looked forward to had been so manifold and so hazardous that when all was done he had a sense of anti-climax, almost of disappointment.

The *Isle of Guernsey* was there, too, on that memorable night, and three days later she went to Newhaven to embark 800 troops. On the 19th she was the second vessel to enter the new port at Arromanches. The *Biarritz*, now thirty years old, which had carried a million leave men during the last war, was not there on D-Day, to the indignation of her crew, but she was there on D+1-Day in a very " sticky " place, and she was shelled when at anchor, while the crew turned on the wireless and Captain Larkins played the mouth organ. Up to August she had made fifteen trips, had been to each of the Normandy beaches and covered 9,000 miles. " Sheer indomitable guts "—the Southern boats, with all the rest of the Armada, had lived up to Captain Payne's phrase.

With that month of August D-Day is definitely past. The follow-up has succeeded the build-up. I have said, tiresomely often, that everything formed part of one vast continuous operation. But there were differences, and one of the most palpable was in the aspect of Southampton Docks. The landing craft had vanished and in their place were large ships loaded with troops or stores ready to follow their smaller comrades as soon as there was a port for them. In time Cherbourg was taken, the town itself surprisingly little damaged, but the port put out of action with German thoroughness, with quay walls blown out, and masses of masonry in the basin to prevent ships from berthing. The Americans did a wonderful work of improvisation by driving piles into the Channel and building staging over the ruined quay walls, and so by August it was possible to land 13,000 tons of stores a day with an almost immediate prospect of 35,000 tons. So now the S.R. train ferry boats, the *Hampton Ferry* and the *Twickenham Ferry*, which had been waiting at Southampton, came into their own and began to carry engines and wagons to France.

They were each fitted with a special gear of monstrous propor-
tions, weighing 258 tons and jutting 35 feet out beyond the vessel's
stern. This may be called a kind of derrick fitted with great straps
for lifting engines, each strap weighing 2½ cwt. For vehicles of less
than 60 tons a ramp was used, and beyond that the derrick, which
could cope with a load of 84 tons and would first lift and turn the
engine and then drop it gently on board. A ferry's full load was
sixteen locomotives, with the engines ready coaled and about twenty
trucks. It could take a whole ambulance train complete with its
personnel, and on her third trip the *Twickenham Ferry* did carry a
hospital train of fourteen coaches and four wagons. She was actually
the first S.R. vessel to enter Cherbourg and was greeted there by a
Free French pilot.

One interesting and cheering point about the *Hampton Ferry*
was the working in perfect harmony of the American Army with the
British Merchant Navy. Beyond the crew the staff of the ship consisted of eighteen American soldiers who were under the direct
command of the ship's Master, Captain Munton. They looked after
the gear, did all the greasing, adjusted the straps for lifting, and they
worked like the most docile of demons.

Cherbourg was our first port, but as the flow of the war was
steadily eastward more and more ports across the Channel fell into
our hands, and with that our own easterly ports became more and
more prominent. Dover and Folkestone began to be something
like their old selves. Early in October a service of coasters laden
with stores and ammunition ran between Dover and Ostend. By
the 8th of November Army mails were carried between the same
two ports. Later in November the *Shepperton Ferry* and the *Twickenham Ferry* were crossing to Calais. On December 7th leave boats
began from Calais to Dover, and on the 8th to Folkestone. Kent
was coming once again into its ancient kingdom.

Leave trains suggest the obvious thought that the D-Day traffic
was not all one way, and as time went on the returning traffic became
steadily heavier and involved a greater strain both on ships and
railways. First there was the bringing back of casualties from the

D-day troops entraining at Waterloo Station

An improvised fire-fighting train with fire pump from a horse-drawn
fire-engine mounted on a tank engine

Allies by the million passed over Southern rails

Tank
th
hund

The famous peacetime sleeping-car Ferries of the S.R., equipped with gantries to help loading, carried thousands of railway engines, coaches, guns and vehicles of all kinds to France

As well as running direct on to the Ferry, the gantry could lift anything up to 84 tons

Continent, for which the entraining points were Southampton Docks, Southampton Terminus, Gosport, Netley, and Cosham. Ambulance trains were also dealt with at Ringwood, Wimborne, Stockbridge, and other stations in the neighbourhood. By June 7th the first casualties were back in this country, and in that month alone there ran 104 ambulance trains, each of which could hold 300 men. In July there were 115 trains, and so this one tributary to the great returning stream flowed on.

The first leave boat had reached Dover early in December, and by the beginning of the new year the leave service began to get into its full stride. Elsewhere I have tried to describe the coming of a leave boat into port, and the sorting out and packing of the men into a leave train, a marvel of quiet, orderly organisation. Dover, Folkestone, and Harwich were the ports for the B.L.A., and Southampton served the U.S. Army. From the beginning of the year till V.E. Day 1,881 leave trains had run to and from the ports and had carried just under 90,000 men. Many of the trains avoided London and ran direct to the provinces or to Scotland, but a large number of men must go to London to catch ordinary trains to their homes. For them the London Passenger Transport Board provided special trains and buses across London, and on certain main line trains carriages were reserved for them in which to continue their journeys. Then there were the prisoners of war to be carried in increasing numbers. A very large proportion were brought here, landing in the main at Southampton Docks and also at Newhaven, Gosport, Tilbury, Purfleet, and Portland. On landing they were first taken to transit camps, the two principal ones being Kempton Park on the Southern and Moreton-in-the-Marsh on the Great Western Railway. Thence after a process of sorting and cleansing they were taken to their permanent abodes, either here or overseas. From D-Day to the end of the year the Southern Railway alone had run 440 trains between the ports and the transit camps, and that may give some clue to a gigantic calculation that shall embrace all the railways and all the time up to the German surrender.

Finally, though this does not belong only to the D-Day period or to one particular railway, there was the conveyance of Army mails,

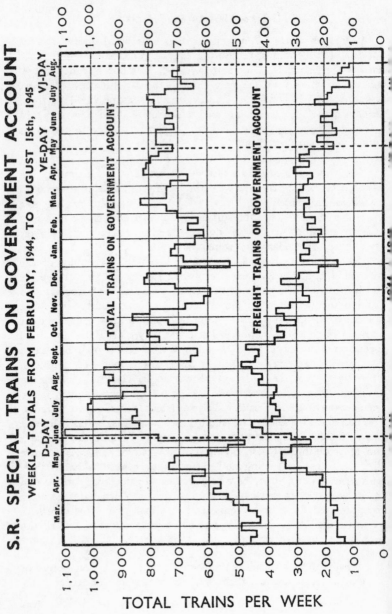

S.R. SPECIAL TRAINS ON GOVERNMENT ACCOUNT

WEEKLY TOTALS FROM FEBRUARY, 1944, TO AUGUST 15th, 1945

TOTAL TRAINS PER WEEK

TOTAL TRAINS ON GOVERNMENT ACCOUNT

FREIGHT TRAINS ON GOVERNMENT ACCOUNT

D-DAY   VE-DAY   VJ-DAY

TOTAL TRAINS PER WEEK

a traffic which grew steadily. The L.M.S. Goods Station at Sutton Park was used by the U.S. Post Office; Canadian mail was sorted first at Manchester and afterwards at Addison Road, Kensington; that for the British forces at Nottingham, from which a special train ran daily to camps in the south. After D-Day it ran first to Tilbury, and later to Dover, carrying letters to our men overseas. Those letters that meant so much may bring to a happy ending this sketch—it can be no more—of a vast, complex and triumphant piece of organisation.

GOVERNMENT WAR SPECIALS —TRAINS AND PERSONNEL

September, 1939, to V.E. Day (May 8th, 1945)

Personnel Duty Trains	30,890
Personnel carried (troops, etc.)	9,367,886
Freight Trains	35,360
Prisoner of War Trains (1944 to V.E. Day) ...	1,127
Prisoners carried...	582,005
Ambulance Trains	1,797
Personnel carried (wounded, staff, etc.) ...	408,051

6,269,160 Service (on duty) Personnel were carried on ordinary trains.

B.E.F. LEAVE TRAINS TO AND FROM PORTS

Number of Trains 1940 1,429		
1945 to V.E. Day ... 1,746		
		3,175
Personnel carried 1940 142,021		
1945 to V.E. Day 845,940	987,961	

Chapter VI

SOME WAR-TIME PROBLEMS

WE, the general public, pay our railways the highest possible compliment in taking them very much for granted. We expect ourselves and our luggage, to say nothing of the multitudinous and mysterious goods that we see in freight trains, to arrive at the right time and the right place and think little or at all of the planning that is needed to get them there. We regard these things as happening in the course of nature. We are a little like Mr. Pecksniff, who believed in the days of his childhood " that pickled onions grew on trees and that every elephant was born with an impregnable castle on his back." Our train is born ready to do our behests. In war time to be sure we did make some allowances and gave a thought now and again to difficulties that must arise. A bomb on the line must clearly be a hindrance. Yet we did not and indeed could not appreciate the number of special problems, or in our now fashionable term " headaches," which the railways had to face. In a general way we still resembled the angry gentleman in an old " Punch " picture who exclaimed, " What! no bread! then bring me some toast." In fact, there was a very large number of these " headaches," some which had been foreseen as war grew ever more inevitable, some which arose and must be dealt with as the tide of war flowed this way or that. I in my turn must now try to deal briefly with a few of them, and I will begin with the rather solid and serious but most essential subject of stores.

STORES
Here is one respect in which perhaps more than in any other we take the railway problems as read. Until in the last war I entered

what is now the Royal Army Ordnance Corps I do not think the question had ever occurred to me how the Army got anything it wanted from a toothbrush to a gun. I may have had some hazy notion derived from old history books that there were people called camp-followers who provided them. Apart from that I supposed that they just grew. I believe this to be a by no means uncommon frame of mind as regards railways, and yet if we ever stopped to think for a moment we should at least faintly realise what a vast amount of stores was needed to keep a railway going, and that more particularly in war time, because many stores depended on imports which with war either came to an end or were much reduced.

To begin with, iron and steel and a number of other things such as cement and tyres were quickly rationed and controlled. As far as iron and steel were concerned the Ministry of Transport made an allocation covering the requirements of all the railway companies, which was then split up between them by mutual consent. As regards the many other stores which the company had hitherto bought how and when it pleased, the inevitable controls, with all possible respect for them, involved a great deal of additional work. It had to be proved to the Controllers that various stores were really and badly wanted, and this often held things up. Again the whole elaborate programme of stores which had been planned ahead had to be changed overnight. Stuff that had been wanted was now no longer wanted, but it had to be kept safe and dry. Then it was wanted for other jobs and handed over accordingly, and when later it was required for its original purpose it just wasn't there. Certain important stores—electric signalling and telephone stores afford one example—had to be greatly increased ; room must be found for them and room was not always easy to find.

Room was indeed a constant problem for one good reason, namely, that stores must be dispersed in view of attack from the air and of the possibility of invasion. Incidentally the Stores Department had itself to be dispersed for a while, but it returned fairly soon to its old home at Waterloo and stayed there. Before the war stores were concentrated in comparatively few depots. Now 32 depots were expanded into about 120. Areas near the coast were clearly not healthy and so stores must be moved, as for example from Newhaven to Lewes, from Dover to Southampton and in certain cases from Southampton to Holmsley.   This plan of dispersal was on the whole very successful, though of course there were accidents.   The depots at Longhedge, at Southampton and at Lower Road, Waterloo, were all more or less damaged and much of the contents lost.   For the new and impromptu ones every kind of building was used—old offices, goods sheds and slaughter houses, a crossing-gate keeper's cottage in the New Forest and the Ladies' Waiting Room at Alresford.   There were even some German vans, complete with the swastika, which had come here in peace time and were now turned into store-houses.   They had to stay at Dover because they would not go through the tunnels.

Then stores need humping, and the young men who were most capable of doing it had gone away on service.   The women did their very best, but they could not physically cope with some of this work and the older men had to shoulder too much of it.   Lifting appliances could not always be obtained and all these problems became harder when stores were dispersed to places where there was no labour to be got.

So much for stores in general.   Now for a very few specially important ones, and the first and most obvious one is coal.   Just by way of introduction, in December, 1940 a water tank above the offices of the coal section was punctured as the result of a bomb, and the rooms were flooded and all papers and books must be salvaged and dried. When the rooms had become habitable again in January, 1941 the whole of their end of the building was destroyed and this time all the papers were destroyed too, but the books were only buried in a strong room and ultimately disinterred.   This is not the sort of thing to make life easier.

Before the war the Company had made its own arrangements with the collieries, chiefly in Kent, Yorkshire and South Wales, the supplies being timed to fall in at different periods.   Generally speaking the war-time supplies were obtained from the same sources as before, but now there was the Ministry of Fuel to say how much could be bought.   The Stores Department have always been on friendly terms with its suppliers and so they remained ; they kept calm and carried on and they never got to the bottom of the bin, but it cannot be denied that they were sometimes frightened.   They were living on a very narrow margin and small, fortuitous things caused anxiety. Even a fog might mean an unpleasant depletion of stocks. The coal was there, but the volume of traffic was so great that it might be hung up for days on the way. With coal, too, as with other stores too many eggs must not be kept in any one basket. Stocks must be drawn away from the invasion area and distributed elsewhere. The number of coal depots on the Southern system rose rapidly to 126 in all. Often one of them would be cleaned out and wagons must be sent to replenish it. And the company had not only to supply its own needs but often those of the Military authorities, R.T.O. offices and Military Guards. There must indeed have been moments when the bottom of the bin came almost peeping through, but there was always just enough coal to cover it.

Oil was likewise an anxiety and the necessary blending of different oils was difficult. Reserves were kept at various strategic points away from the invasion area and the normal reserve was doubled from two weeks' to one month's supply. Petrol rationing, too, meant forms and coupons, an additional labour with which the layman can sympathize.

Timber, chiefly for sleepers, crossings and rolling stock, was another of the urgent needs often hard to meet. The Stores Department had seen the war coming and had laid in a big stock of timber, a prescience it had cause to bless. Sleepers are as a rule made of a certain red wood from Poland; that source was instantly at an end and its place taken by Canada. Experiments had been made before the war with concrete sleepers, but these were not a success since they would not stand the constant shock. Practically all imported timber came under the heading of " National Stocks " and there was the sternest supervision over its supply. Railway timber stocks were often pooled and so one Company was able to help another. Home grown timber became extremely valuable and the oak came to some extent into its old war-time kingdom, not now for ships but for railway wagons.

Then there was the question of what the ordinary person would call tarpaulins but which I now know should be called wagon sheets. In peace time the Southern has not, comparatively speaking, a large goods traffic, but in war this increased out of knowledge and so did the number of wagon sheets needed. Normally these are made of flax and hemp and they last a long time. Here was another source dried up ; Indian cotton had to be used instead and this does not remain waterproof for long and tears easily. A sheet's working life was reduced from five to two and a half years. Thus not only were many more sheets needed but many more repairs.

There was clothing too ; there was not enough cloth available to make the staff uniforms. The company gets its uniforms made in complete suits in the East end of London, which suffered so greatly in the air raids. The actual factories escaped but the employees' houses were in many cases destroyed or damaged, and it is one of the lessons of the air war that work depends largely on the workmen having somewhere to live. It was a sad blow when a quantity of new uniforms that had just been delivered were destroyed by a bomb before they could be issued. And here again there was the additional complexity of coupons.

Everybody knows from personal experience what a problem stationery became during the war, and the Railway Company, a prodigal devourer of paper in ordinary times, was therefore a great sufferer. New states of things have odd and unsuspected repercussions and here is an example ; the restriction on road transport naturally increased the goods traffic by rail and so the demand for wagon labels ; from August to December, 1939, as compared with the same period in 1938 the demand increased by 85 per cent. As to envelopes, the Company had to devise fully as many economical dodges as did the humblest individual, and the consumption of new ones was reduced by two millions a year. As an illustration of this economy, the file which I am consulting as I write is typed on pieces of the backs of old posters as to cheap day excursions, with pictures of the " beauty spots " of Kent.

Finally besides all these stores which were normally needed, the Department was faced with demands for a variety of things that had never been wanted before. Of such were 2,000 straw palliasses for the Home Guard, the Police and the Firewatchers ; rope rings to support the Home Guards' tripods ; sacks stuffed with straw for their bayonet exercises, and aprons made from salved tarpaulins for the women carriage cleaners, who found that the acid they used burnt holes in their clothes.

SALVAGE

This seems a good place to say a word on a subject germane to that of stores, salvage. From the beginning the Company tried its hardest to prevent waste and to rescue valuable scrap in every possible direction. A film called " Saving our Scrap " was made and produced by Southern men and women and shown all over the system in a mobile cinematographic coach. In September of 1940 the Company could announce that in one month 4,000 tons of miscellaneous salvage had been disposed of. Over 3,000 tons of iron and steel consisted of old rails and chairs ; 200 tons of an old hydraulic power plant now grown obsolete, and there were heating pipes, girders, boilers and even a rolling mill from the Works at Ashford. Straw, rope and twine, bottles and bones and broken glass—all was grist that came to the Salvage Officers' mill. In the course of the year 1940 45,000 miscellaneous tons had been collected and in 1941 retrieved waste paper alone was responsible for nearly 1,000 tons. For some part of this the passengers could claim credit, for every station had a waste paper basket on a grand scale with a fevered appeal as to newspapers, magazines and cigarette packets. Some inspired person, adapting a well-known remark of the Iron Duke's, declared that the battle of Europe would be won on the salvage dumps of Waterloo.

DECENTRALISATION

The principle of keeping important eggs in separate baskets has already been referred to in describing the dispersal of stores, and it was also applied to the Administrative Officers of the Company. Some time before the war the Southern, like the other railway companies, had taken over buildings in the country where administration could be carried on if London were bombed. This emergency head-quarters was at Deepdene near Dorking. It is a large and imposing country house, which had lately been used as an hotel, in a green and peaceful spot, and it has in its grounds a cave dug in the face of a hill, which was developed into a catacomb full of tables and telephones so that work could be carried on whatever happened overhead. A house at Elmstead Woods in Kent was taken for further offices and part of the old locomotive works at Brighton set aside for the same purpose. In addition there were Divisional headquarters instituted at Woking, Redhill and Orpington, each with its reinforced underground chamber for the control staff.

So when war broke out there began a game of " general post " on a grand and complex scale, and this game, as far as many depart-. ments were concerned, continued to be played throughout the war. I have before me an elaborate record of all the moves and counter-moves, but if I could wholly grasp them I would not inflict them on the reader. It must be enough to indicate a very few. The General Manager and a number of his staff took up their quarters at Deepdene while some stayed at Waterloo, and there were moves between the two from time to time. Gradually as the war progressed more and more came back to Waterloo and the General Manager himself divided his time between the two places, holding conferences every week with those who remained at Deepdene. The Chief Civil Engineer and the Traffic Manager were permanently at Deepdene. Stores after a brief sojourn in the country returned to Waterloo and so did Public Relations. The Solicitor presumably said " J'y suis, j'y reste " and remained at Waterloo all the time. The three Divisional Superintendents for London East, Central and West moved to their " battle headquarters " at Orpington, Woking and Redhill respectively and stayed there. The Divisional Officers at Southampton Central stayed where they were, sending their documents to Andover by train every night, except when owing to damage from raids, they had to take refuge in railway coaches at Salisbury. Those at Exeter " stayed put." And this very brief account, which leaves out innumerable moves of innumerable and important people, is as much as my brain, and possibly the reader's, can stand. Several special trains were made ready as offices but the only one that had to be used was that already mentioned when temporarily evicted Southampton must go to Salisbury.

One thing is clear, that this game of complicated moves must have involved a great deal of complicated communication between different departments, and this seems the place to mention the use of wireless. It was obvious that there must be, as in fact there sometimes were, great difficulties when telephones were put out of action by air raids and, in the early days at any rate, there was the imminent and practical fear of invasion. There were first of all wireless sets at Deepdene, Orpington, Redhill and Woking and later three more at Southampton, Exeter and Salisbury. It was later decided to make no more " fixed " stations but to install wireless sets, including those which had already been set up, in 10 cwt. motor parcel vans, which could act as mobile transmitter stations. These vans were kept at suitable places as near as might be to the various divisional headquarters, in order to avoid the enemy from plotting the whereabouts of the divisional offices. They were of great value in transmitting railway messages. Orpington for instance dealt with as many as forty outward and fifteen inward messages every day, and the installation in the west was peculiarly useful during the days following the severe " Baedeker " raid on Exeter in the spring of 1942.

There was another means of communication, the Emergency Road Service, of the greatest value and calling for much fortitude and endurance in its members. It was maintained all round the clock day in and day out throughout the war. That such a service would be needed had been foreseen before the war began ; seven secondhand motor cycles had been obtained, a number of cars had been lent by members of the staff and a band of volunteers recruited to drive them. On the 2nd of September, 1939 began the first of many circular trips, connecting the headquarters at Deepdene with the three battle headquarters at Orpington, Redhill and Woking. When the service was at full strength and fairly in its stride there were 33 despatch riders based at Deepdene with 26 cars and 14 motor cycles, and seven at each of the battle headquarters with a corresponding number of cars and cycles. Each man had to be capable of driving either the one or the other and each took his appointed turn of duty through the twenty-four hours. It was a hard life, in which many of the men could only see their homes occasionally, sometimes at long intervals. It involved at best many a cold wet journey in bitter weather and at worst the gravest danger from air raids which was never allowed to deter the messenger from carrying out his mission. These missions were of various sorts, some of them of a routine order in the regular carrying of urgent despatches from Deepdene to the Main London stations, others undertaken on the spur of the moment, such as taking a specialist as quickly as possible to deal with damage or dislocation caused by air raids. Drivers and Firemen were often taken from their trains to their homes and conversely relief men brought from home to train. When one job was over there was often another that had suddenly arisen and was waiting to be done. The more thickly the bombs were falling the greater the likelihood of some such impromptu task. Right through the heaviest times of the blitz in London a car left Deepdene every night for New Cross to undertake any trip required there, and it is something to be truly proud of that no single despatch rider ever turned his back on a job. As may be imagined all sorts of exciting and sometimes hair-raising things befell them. They ran over hose pipes, over mattresses and furniture scattered about the road, sometimes over heaps of bricks. One man, driving without lights, found his wheels suddenly dipping into a bomb crater. Another saw the tram lines on the road blown up in front of his nose, while he himself was blown off his motor cycle. Shrapnel and flying gravel or glass were all in the day's work, and dismounting to lie down flat on the ground and then getting up to go on again was a comparatively common experience. Trains might be stopped and telephones break down but the despatch service carried on, if not by one road then by another, and with an unflagging spirit.

THE SOUTHERN'S SALVAGE DRIVE

Waste Material Saved
totalled 263,297 Tons comprising

Various Metals	255,379 tons
Paper	5,397 ,,
Straw	1,282 ,,
Textiles, Rope and Twine	1,115 ,,
Rubber	124 ,,

Old Razor Blades
collected at stations from members of the public and staff totalled 3,290,000. (The sale of these blades realised £847 for the R.A.F. Benevolent Fund)

Chapter VII

MORE WAR-TIME PROBLEMS

RAILWAY LIAISON OFFICERS

THE Southern was the only railway in the country to institute Railway Liaison Officers—further evidence, if indeed more be wanted, of how conspicuously it was in the forefront of the battle. After Dunkirk this country passed clearly into a defensive phase; there was a time when there might be a landing almost any day and it was vitally important that the railways and the defending troops should be in closest possible contact. With the best intentions on both sides, however, that contact was not at first easy to make. In every district there was somebody called " The Competent Military Authority," but from a railway point of view he had some of the qualities of the Elusive Pimpernel. He might be a sailor or a soldier or a marine. To the district railway superintendent anxious to find him it seemed at times that he might be anybody or anywhere.

The essential point was to get in touch with him and so on the 5th of July, 1940, the Traffic Manager went to Hounslow and met two most helpful Brigadiers to whom he made his proposal. It was just at the time of the splitting of one command into two, the South Eastern and the Southern, and the headquarters of the new South Eastern Command was then at Tunbridge Wells. The Traffic Manager's suggestion was that there should be a railwayman attached to this headquarters. Further, as the French Railways had failed from too much centralisation, and decentralisation must now be the motto, he wanted a railwayman at the headquarters of every division that had to guard the coast.

General Thorne then had the South Eastern Command and the railway very gratefully remembers him, for he entered wholeheartedly into the project which thereupon became a fact. There were several good men available from the Continental Department since their occupation was temporarily gone. Others were produced somehow and from somewhere. All were most kindly received in the various headquarter messes ; they gained the soldiers' confidence and the association was as friendly as it was valuable. There were various ways in which this railway liaison officer could be of value. Whatever problem whether of traffic or engineering arose, and they were always arising, he could instantly put his hand on the appropriate specialist to deal with it. The soldiers were fertile in ideas as to defensive measures for the railways in case of invasion ; the R.L.O. could tell them which were technically workable and which were not, and above all he could insist with all his energies on one great principle " Keep the lines clear."

When the scheme had been set on its legs at Tunbridge Wells the Traffic Manager went on his missionary enterprise to Salisbury and found the Southern Command equally ready to co-operate. Thus in time there were Railway Liaison Officers all the way from Dover to Cornwall. And here we light on the names of two most distinguished soldiers. In course of time General Thorne was succeeded by General (as he then was) Montgomery and he, like his predecessor, did everything he could to help. General Alexander succeeded to the Southern Command and was of the greatest assistance in getting the system to work. It is pleasant to associate these two famous names with the Southern story.

At one time there were in all nineteen of these Railway Liaison Officers, with the two at Aldershot and Salisbury respectively exercising a general control over their respective areas. While they existed they had almost innumerable functions. In particular they must keep the Command to which they belonged informed of any measures for blocking the railway in case of emergency and tell every station master in the area who was his " Competent Military

Authority," the right R.T.O. with whom to communicate and the nearest unit to which any stranded soldier should be sent if there was a general recall from leave. They must tell railway headquarters of rail tank blocks and wagon blocks and of the bridges prepared for demolition by the military authorities. They must always be provided with a despatch rider on a motor cycle in case the telephone broke down. They must in general always be ready for the signal " Stand to " which was an " Alert " and for " Action Stations " which meant imminent peril of invasion. Military exercises meant much labour in the working out of complex time tables and Christmas and Easter leave was another problem. In exchange the Liaison Officers were able to get valuable help from the soldiers in the winter storms which played havoc with signals and telephone wires. Apart from the military Liaison Officers others were appointed to keep in touch with the Consultative Transport Committee set up in case of emergency at important centres by the Regional Transport Commissions. On these committees there was always a railway representative and it was the duty of these Road Transport Liaison Officers to report daily to the Commissions any dislocation of traffic caused by enemy action. The R.L.O's had been appointed primarily in case of invasion. As that possibility first diminished and then vanished so they were for the most part disbanded, but they had admirably served their turn.

DECENTRALISING FOOD STOCKS

Before the outbreak of war the Ministry of Home Security had planned the storing of food in various places in case communications should be cut and the inhabitants have to live for a while on their own fat. These food stocks came under three heads, and three different schemes, National Reserves, Emergency Dumps and Evacuee Emergency Rations. The places chosen were often on railway property and the stores were kept in various buildings—sheds, offices, stables and old coaches. As soon as war was declared the Ministry of Food sent canned meat, canned milk, wheat and flour, biscuits, chocolate and tinned fruit to these prearranged sites, and this involved considerable traffic on the Southern Railway. Redhill housed flour and biscuits ; Caterham had a large stock of corned beef, so had Ewell ; at Tunbridge Wells all sorts of food was kept in the Company's stables and in different places in the town ; indeed this was probably for a while the largest store in the country. That was in 1939 and in 1940 came a considerable change with the tide of war and the collapse of France. Kent was no longer a good place for keeping too large a stock. Folkestone clearly was not, and its stock must be moved. The same remark applied to Ashford which had become in effect a front line town. Again, many people had been evacuated from London to rural Kent and since they must now be moved elsewhere there was a corresponding movement of stores. There was a general flow from the coast and in a westerly direction.

In the west there were created a number of what were called buffer depots, to which food could be moved from the ports, chiefly from Avonmouth and Newport (Monmouth). The Office of Works requisitioned the places of storage and the railway moved the food there. As a rule these places were in quiet country neighbourhoods but a number of small depots were scattered over the city of Exeter. The Southern Railway deservedly acquired much merit with the Divisional Food Controller over this scheme, for it not only carried the stores by rail and if necessary by road transport as well, but also undertook the stacking of them, and a great Panjandrum from the Ministry of Food said that theirs was the best stacking he had seen. Up to the 20th of January, 1941 the Southern staff at Exeter had tackled 10,000 tons of food. Some of this work had moreover to be done on the spur of the moment and without warning. Bristol for instance had been having a bad time and might have a worse; so it was decided to move ten lorry loads of food to Exeter. The food arrived on a Saturday night when nearly all the men were off duty. The word went forth that the lorries must either be unloaded or they must be sent back to Bristol. The food Controller did not appeal in vain and despite all the difficulties of the black-out the men were forthcoming and the lorries unloaded.

GOVERNMENT COAL DUMPS

A kindred subject is that of the Government Coal Dumps which were scattered over the Southern system. It was early in 1940 that the Minister of Mines proposed to the railway companies that these dumps should be placed at various strategic points, in case communications were interrupted, the coal to be used only in an emergency. Many sites were chosen though by no means all of them were used,

With broom sticks for guns and no uniform, all ranks of Railway Staff joined the Local Defence Volunteers (later Home Guard) in June, 1940. A Guards N.C.O. instructs at Waterloo

Tank trap testing before erecting traps at many points on the Southern

S.R. Home Guard manning a light anti-aircraft gun

Heavy mobile guns near the coast on the Dover line

but there was a very considerable number of dumps, most of them in goods yards. Kent and Sussex, especially Kent, had most of them, ranging, to mention but a few, from Canterbury, Paddock Wood and Faversham to Penge, Sidcup and other stations near London. Some of the western dumps were at Hewish, Delabole, Exmouth, Fremington, Dorchester and Millbrook. The coal arrived from Northern collieries in blocks of between twenty and thirty wagons and, having been carried by the railway, was stacked by local contractors.

A certain number of special trains was needed but the greater part of the traffic was by ordinary freight service. In multiplicity and variety of dumps Southampton seems to have held first place. It had dumps for the Southampton Corporation, for the Ministry of Mines, for the boat service to and from the Isle of Wight, for the Ministry of War Transport, for the Admiralty, for the locomotives of the Southern Railway and, apart from all this stacked coal, there was a large quantity kept in barges in the various basins at the Docks.

DEFENCE PRECAUTIONS

While these and many other war time measures were being taken and problems foreseen, with at least one eye on invasion, there were some other things happening still more secret. They would then have seemed to us had we known of them exceedingly ominous. To-day they can be " revealed " to the agreeable curdling of our blood.

The Ashford Works were hard at it making armour plating for twelve armoured trains to be used on the various railway systems in the country. The Southern had four of such patrol trains, one based at Canterbury, one at Tonbridge, one at Barnstaple and one at Wadebridge. Each train consisted of a tank engine with a runner wagon on either side of it and at each end a 20 ton armoured truck equipped with a light calibre gun which could be used for anti-aircraft purposes. Each had anti-grenade nets and gun carriers and a store of reserve ammunition at its stabling point. The trains were controlled by a military group and the enginemen and guards, all railwaymen in civilian life, came from a military operating unit. Their purposes were threefold, to patrol the line for observation, to protect railwaymen engaged on repairs, and if necessary to form rallying points in defence for the soldiers or the Home Guard. They were

kept continuously in steam and made patrolling trips at intervals
travelling at about 25 miles an hour.   Here was another case in which
as time went on precautions against invasion could be relaxed, and
by the late summer of 1943 the trains patrolled no more.

Another precaution still more sinister was the placing of " super
heavy " batteries at various points on the line which may now be set
out, in order to heighten our sense of gratitude that they were never
needed : Aldington, Bishopsbourne, Adisham, Kingsnorth (between
Ham Street and Appledore, Rolvenden, Shepherdswell, Eythorne,
Staple, Poulton, Lydden and Martin Mill.   In some cases the batteries
were accompanied by a living train ; in others the men lived in
billets.   Diesel engines were used.   At several places new sidings
had to be made for the living trains ; a new connecting single line
between the line from Faversham to Canterbury East and that from
Ashford to Canterbury West was made solely for this purpose.   These
batteries were intended primarily to fire at the beaches but might have
been used to fire at other points from the running lines.   They might
also in circumstances possible but not pleasant to contemplate have
moved further back to other sites.

There was likewise a number of ambulance and casualty evacuation trains which moved hither and thither on the Southern system
according to circumstances.   There were five emergency railheads for them and an alternative to each rail-head in case
of accidents.   There was a number of other stations at which
ambulance trains could be dealt with if necessary at a particular siding
or platform previously ascertained.   During the early days of the
war casualty evacuation trains were berthed at Tunbridge Wells.
Subsequently there were two at Sevenoaks, manned night and day,
and often used to move hospital patients from dangerous areas to the
west of England.   Tattenham Corner, Hassocks and Earley were
other berths.   After the fall of France there had been four ambulance
trains at Bournemouth West and two at Romsey, but these subsequently
left and were, as far as the west was concerned, kept on Great Western
territory.

IN THE BLACK-OUT

I have kept to the end something as to which we can all appreciate
and sympathise with the railways' difficulties because of our personal
experiences.   That is the black-out.   We were all more or less

" afraid to go home in the dark " and did our best to avoid it, but here are few who had not to do it now and then, and it would be an abuse of language to say that it was either comfortable or agreeable. In the earliest days of the war the passenger's object was threefold, to find his way along the platform without running into other people, to find a seat in a carriage and not on some invisible person's lap, and to find his station at the other end. The Railway Company had to do its best to help him in these respects but it had if possible even graver pre-occupations. There is a great deal of important railway work to be done at night-time necessitating at least some measure of light, such as that of the marshalling yards, the working of locomotive depots and the dealing with parcels and mails. Long before the war broke out experiments had been made and a certain very modest standard of lighting called " Category B," which was practically invisible from the air and so could be maintained during air raids, had been decided on. So modest was it that for many purposes it proved almost useless and there arose " Category C " which could be used by permission of the police if it was absolutely essential and could be instantly put out in case of an air raid warning. The problem of dimming stations was a most laborious one. Electric light bulbs and gas globes had to be sprayed with blue on a scale so large that a special spraying plant must be made for the purpose.

Now as to the passenger in his compartment, it will be remembered that at first a stygian blackness prevailed and voices came to him out of the dark from those whom he never saw unless by the flash of a torch. By the beginning of October, 1939, blue electric bulbs began to be installed ; they did not allow of reading but gave a ghastly and distorted vision of the other occupants. It was a small mercy but one for which travellers showed their gratitude by stealing the bulbs in such quantities that a reward had to be offered for their conviction. Meanwhile there were more experiments and by November white lighting had been introduced in some Southern trains, both steam and electric. These lights were extinguished by a master switch in case of air raids and this became one of the duties of a new official. This was the train-lighting attendant who turned on the blue lamps when the white ones went out, shut windows and pulled down blinds a quarter of an hour before black-out time and patrolled the train to see that rules were observed. At the same time there appeared in every carriage the familiar notice " During Black-out hours---for your own safety keep all blinds down " and so on. The work was steadily carried on and what a task it was may be judged from the fact that the equipment needed for a single main line coach included 20 shades, 45 blinds and 2 lbs. of black-out paint. By 1943 " improved " train lighting was complete and in September, 1944, with the tide of victory flowing further and further west, came a great moment when normal lighting was restored in all trains, except in brake vans. The blinds must still be drawn, however, and lights put out on the sounding of an alert. On April 24th, 1945, peace time lighting was allowed everywhere but in coastal areas and there began the considerable if cheering job of taking the black-out paint off the windows. It took about ten minutes work with a safety razor blade to clean one window and there were 300,000 to be cleaned.

Lastly there was the agonising problem of getting out at the right station. Some delightful verses by Mr. A. A. Milne in " Punch " summed it up to admiration and I take leave to quote the last verse—

> We were alone, I hailed the fellow blindly,
> " Excuse me, sir, I live at Wavertree.
> Is it the next but one ? " *She* answered kindly
> " It was the last but three."

A great many years earlier " Punch " had had an unkind picture called " Puzzle. Find the name of the station," but great steps forward had been made since then and now with the war they must be retraced. It was no longer permissible to illuminate the name and an unlighted name became invisible at night. Still worse was to come, for with the fall of France there was the danger of enemy parachutists who must not know where they were when they landed. One example of the extreme precautions taken will be familiar to all who travelled to and from Charing Cross. A public house visible from the line called " The Hero of Waterloo " was suddenly truncated and became " The Hero of." The large name boards to be normally found at every station vanished, since they might be seen by the low-flying aircraft ; lamp signs and even seat signs had to go the same way. Certain modifications were allowed, since life must go on, and, briefly, signs were allowed under cover and where they could not be seen from the highway or if seen could not be understood. One ingenious device was that of putting a series of names in letters one inch high so that they formed a frieze at eye level; it was hoped that even in the black-out these would be visible with the help of torches, but torches were prohibited during air raids. Then somebody had a notion among notions. Up to this time all station names in whatever form had as a matter of course been placed parallel with the line. Why not have a board at right angles with it ? This could be put under the covered way and lighted in accordance with the rules. Anyone could see it by leaning out of the window, except perhaps those at the end of a very long train and those in the one carriage exactly opposite the board. Leatherhead was the station chosen for the experiment to be inspected by the Minister of Transport, the Chairman of the Railway Executive Committee and the General Manager. They came, they saw, they were conquered, and more such sign boards were made to the greater comfort of the passenger. There ought to be a useful future for them even though the black-out is now only a memory, for the great thing in finding a name is to know where to look for it and these right angle signs have far fewer rivals to distract the eye than have the parallel ones.

EMERGENCY SIGNS AND TRAVEL KIOSKS

The name of his station is only one of the many things that a passenger wants to be told. There are numberless other notices in the station that direct him this way and that and there is perhaps nothing that he takes so entirely for granted. But these notices have to be written or printed or painted and with war imminent it became clear that the need for many new ones would suddenly arise. So towards the end of August, 1939, a section was formed at Waterloo to provide them and it worked the clock round. A.R.P., Air Raid Shelters, First Aid, No Smoking and R.T.O.—these are obvious examples of notices that now began to appear. There was " Danger Gas " also, but that never was wanted. There were many minor ones, such as notices telling of alternative routes after air raids, and emergency time tables. Many of them had to be written by hand there and then. Later came notices as to where to form queues, as for taxis. These various signs were chiefly needed at the London termini, but many other stations wanted them too, including the small name signs when larger lettering was disallowed, and all these demands were met by the section. They had plenty to keep them going in shifts throughout the twenty-four hours.

We of the travelling public always have a good many questions to ask and if our own are of course " really necessary " those of other people seem sometimes superflous, especially now that the unseen announcer, apparently in the roof, tells us so much by loudspeaker. It is a matter in which we are acutely conscious of one another's little weaknesses. In war time, however, there inevitably arose a number of questions that really did need asking and answering. Especially in the time of air raids the problem of alternative routes was a constant one. Soldiers fresh from overseas naturally wanted to know how to get to their homes. So during the blitz in 1940 the giving of advice to travellers was systematically organised, primarily to help travellers when lines were blocked by bomb damage. Enquiry kiosks were set up on the Southern not only at all the London termini but at some fifteen suburban stations as well. The staff at each kiosk were kept up-to-date as to all train alterations on the line. They had the latest information by telephone from the various control offices and if the telephone broke down it was brought to them by a despatch rider. They had also the invaluable A.B.C. guide to help travellers as far as might be on their journeys over other lines. And they earned their living by the sweat of their brows. During the week ending December 13th, 1941, a census was taken of the enquiries at the one and twenty kiosks in the London area and the total was, according to my arithmetic, 22,486. Charing Cross came first with over 4,500 and Waterloo a good second with over 3,700, but the suburban stations did nobly too with Wimbledon 1,139, Sutton 1,443 and Woolwich 1,505. Oddly enough the two lowest totals came from two London stations, Blackfriars and Holborn Viaduct. That the travellers at those two stations were so independent, or so incurious may seem odd, but the reason probably was that they were nearly all season-ticket holders and therefore well acquainted with the line. Those figures are sufficiently impressive but I must give just two more. In 1944 Charing Cross reached its peak with 8,000 questions answered in a week and during the same time the Central Telephone Enquiry Bureau at Waterloo answered 21,785.

WAR-TIME WORKS

Total new track miles laid down (running lines and sidings) 123
New stations and halts erected 6

Signal Boxes

New Signal boxes built 35
New ground frames built 43
Number of vital boxes and overline boxes given overhead
protection 19
Number of timber boxes strengthened 28

Air Raid Shelters and Strong Points

(a) Major strong points
H.I. (Heavy Incendiary) Shelters 9
Battle Headquarters 3
Control Centres 12

(b) Air Raid Shelters
Sand-bag protection to existing buildings ; strengthening of
cellars ; " open-dive " trenches, steel lined trenches, pre-
cast concrete trenches ; brick built shelters and steel
shelters 1,723

Glass removed from Railway Premises   Sq. ft. 2,200,000

New Emergency Depots

For Permanent Way and Bridging material 18
For Signal and Telegraph material 18

Wireless

Fixed stations 15
Mobile stations 5

Telephone

New Telephone Exchanges 35
New Telephone Circuits ... ... 2,605 pair miles

Canteens

Staff Canteens, Mobile Canteens and Trailer Kitchens 37

Anti-Tank Rail Barriers 283

Chapter VIII

AT THE WORKS

THE Southern Railway has four main works, Eastleigh in Hampshire, Brighton and Lancing in Sussex, and Ashford in Kent. Before the railway amalgamation, works served, as it were, as maids of all work for their respective lines; they were self-sufficient in themselves. Afterwards they were able to pool their resources of industry so that each could devote itself to a particular branch. To-day, for instance, Eastleigh is primarily the home of the locomotive, Ashford of the freight wagon, and Lancing of the carriage.

Purely as regards railway jobs—and there were many others to be done—the war brought a great strain of work and necessitated certain changes and expansions in the Works. After the amalgamation of 1923, and with the extension of electrification, the Brighton Works, which had been originally opened in 1852, may almost be said to have been closed. In 1928 much of the work done there was transferred to Eastleigh and Ashford, while Brighton was used only for running repairs. Of the seven acres of buildings, three and a half were unused; there were about eighteen machines in the Works. With the war the Works must be expanded to deal with special war jobs; machinery which had been out of use for years was transferred from Eastleigh and Ashford to Brighton; sixty-six new machines were installed from outside sources, thirty-four from other depots. Brighton began to hum again and in 1943, for instance, thirty large locomotives were built. At the outbreak of war 253 men were employed there; by the end of 1943 there were 755 men, 214 women working full time and 38 women half time.

And here, apropos of engines, let me interpolate one word which is perhaps a little irrelevant but not to be resisted. Right through the war the ceremony has been maintained of formally christening the new engines the Company has built. It is such a pleasant one that I cannot leave it out. The one I saw myself took place after war had ended but the rite was exactly the same as it had been throughout. My engine, if I may so term it, was one of the " Merchant Navy " class locomotives, designed for a dual war-time purpose of pulling great loads whether of passengers or freight. Each of them is called after some famous steamship line, most of them associated with Southampton Docks, and the first of them all was very properly the " Channel Packet " after the Southern's own boats.

It is a very simple ceremony, and yet a moving one. There, drawn up at one of the Waterloo platforms, seventy feet from end to end, is the newly-born monster, squat, crouching and formidable and yet with something of innocent, youthful pride in its fresh green and gold. In my ignorance I could wish it had a visible funnel but that is because I am used to funnels and not because they are in themselves beautiful. In front of one small part of its side there is a mysterious curtain. The Chairman makes a little speech ; so does the Chairman of the Shipping Line. Then he draws aside the curtain and behold ! behind it is the line's house flag flaming scarlet on the green background. The engine pulls out and attaches itself to a waiting train, since it is now to tackle its first job. Directors and officials stand at the end of the platform watching. As the mighty creature slowly gathers speed they shout " Good Luck " to the driver, who touches his cap and grins back at them. The long train vanishes into the distance and one more engine has begun its working life in the railway's service.

Railway work was very far from being all that was done in the Works. Before the war had actually begun it had been realised that for the task of rearmament these Works with their shops and machinery and equipment were immensely valuable in the making of all sorts of munitions. There came orders steadily increasing with the magnitude of the war from the Ministry of Supply, the Admiralty, the War Office and the Air Ministry, while at the same time the railways became in certain respects sub-contractors to the armament makers. The railway shops were like a man playing on a pair of kettledrums, turning now to their normal, increasing, and more than ever imperative work, and then to the new and special tasks which the war had thrust upon them. Between the two it may be imagined that they were up to the pin of their collar. I must later enumerate a few of the additional tasks, many of them at the time they were undertaken profound secrets, to which these four Works set themselves. At the present moment I must try to say something of one of them in particular, Ashford, which can stand for the other three. I choose it both because I passed a most thrilling day there and because it was in war time essentially a front line town.

In itself it is a pleasant old market town, the mart of Romney sheep from time long past; but it is also, as to a large fraction of its population, a railway town. The railway men live mainly in what is called the New Town, houses built by the railway company at different dates and grouped chiefly round a pretty, triangular piece of green. A large part of the Works themselves may be said to lie in a triangle bounded by the line to Dover, the line to Hastings and the River Stour. The wagon works are beyond the Hastings line.

Ashford is only twelve miles as the crow flies from Dover; it was only seven minutes flying time distant from the German airfields in France. Try as you will, and all that was possible in the way of camouflage was done, you cannot hide such a place, with the railway lines guiding the enemy planes to it like so many homing pigeons. It was a most obviously vulnerable spot, and the work had to be done in the most trying and nerve-wearing conditions. It would not have been surprising if attacks had been so constant and destructive as to force the Works to shut down. In all the circumstances it escaped with merciful lightness. It had a very hard time, as witness the fact that it had 2,881 red warnings and 2,044 spotters' warnings. Many of the red warnings did not materialize but the warnings given by the spotters, perched in a high place above the Works, were in a different category. These spotters, all men who had their normal work to do and undertook this additional task in shifts, had their own sirens and did a very fine job. They could and did give the vital minute or two of warning. Three minutes was in fact on the average all the time they could give, but they were only once beaten and that through no fault of their own. That time enemy planes appeared suddenly from behind a low hill only two or three miles away, and the sounding of the sirens and the dropping of the bombs were simultaneous. With time so crucial, there must be shelters everywhere for everybody, and there were. A few were partly underground but most of them were above ground, brick buildings dotted here and there on the floors of the shops. There was no man or woman anywhere in the Works who could not reach a shelter in one minute. At the beginning, before the spotters' warnings, conditions were a little chaotic, some people staying in shelter during a red warning, others coming out to work, and a good deal of time being necessarily wasted. Once the spotters had been instituted and people had gained complete faith in them, as they soon did, work went on bravely with the absolute minimum of stoppages.

All things are comparative and Ashford may be said to have got off cheaply, but it endured nine serious raids and it had a certain number, not a large one, of unfortunate people killed. To walk through the shops to-day is to see certain new clean patches against the darker colour of the original building, which tell their tale. At one place in the wagon works I stood on the spot where a man saw a bomb bouncing straight at him, when it capriciously broke back and he, as he said, " legged it " behind a pile of timber, just in time before the bomb exploded. Things might have been much worse but think of over 2,000 spotters' warnings in five and a half years ! Does it not sound a desperately continuous and cumulative strain ? As far as the flying bombs were concerned there was relatively not much to complain of, but still they were continuously passing over Ashford's head with our fighters attacking them, and that may have been exciting but cannot have been pleasant. I heard a siren at Ashford but it was only blowing the familiar " All clear " note for the dinner hour. I should have thought that even dinner would not make it a wholly agreeable sound.

In the Heavy Machine Shop, the Erecting Shop and so on, there are many miraculous and seductive machines cutting pieces of steel into intricate patterns with more than human neatness and precision, drilling, welding, making showers of sparks compared with which

fireworks must " pale their ineffectual fires," and so on ; but they
are not specially war-like and so I will not describe them, supposing
that I could. There are likewise many engines, either suffering from
some definite ailment or having come in for overhaul after some vast
number of miles, more or less as a matter of routine. They are
ingeniously manœuvred by turntables, each into its particular stall.
Some of them need but little doctoring, but others must be stripped
almost to their very foundations and put together again.

These things constitute the daily round, but there is one shop,
not a very large one, not comparable in outward impressiveness with
another very nearly a quarter of a mile long, which possesses an
altogether outstanding and war-like record. I christened it in my
own mind, Joe Stalin's shop. That is not an irreverence, I trust,
towards the great Russian leader, because it was largely admiration
for him and his people that urged the workers in that shop to
altogether extraordinary exertions. The order received in the
autumn of 1941 was for 1,000 open 13-ton freight wagons for Russia,
and it was completed in less than ten weeks. The fervour of enthusiasm
which filled the shop was astonishing. Russian flags fluttered,
Russian slogans were chalked up. If for a single moment a single
man seemed to be taking life easily he was urged on by his fellows
with " Come on ! Old Joe wants that one." All worked double
shifts night and day, and produced double the usual output in each
shift. There were 76 raid warnings during the ten weeks but they
could not interrupt the work. 130 men, 19 boys and 22 women
averaged 67 hours work a week for the whole job. They were
neither to hold nor to bind.

These wagons were to be sent in sections to the Middle East
Forces. There they were to be assembled and put into service to
convey war materials by way of the Persian Gulf to our Russian
Allies. Every wagon contained 792 parts and each part was numbered
to correspond with photographs which had been sent ahead for the
purpose of assembling them. On the 10th of November, Colonel
Llewellin, then Parliamentary Secretary to the Minister of War
Transport, came down to Ashford and drove the last nail into the last
packing crate. He drove it with an American hammer to symbolize
the unity of the three Allied Nations. When the wagons arrived at

their destination they were erected at the rate of three quarters of an hour apiece, by a unit that had no workshop facilities, a limited number of trained artisans and no wagon-builders on its establishment. It was only twenty working weeks from the day of beginning work on the first wagon till that on which the last was in service, 12,000 route miles away from its source. That was delivering the goods with a vengeance. " Old Joe " got his wagons in record time.

Ashford did not have long to rest on its laurels after this frantic spurt. At the beginning of December came another order for 600 12-ton open goods wagons, with screw couplings and the French type of Westinghouse brakes, to be shipped overseas. The work began on December 4th, 1941, and on the last day of the year the last wagon was complete. That was an average of a little over twenty-one wagons a day, another great achievement.

That historic shop, the birthplace of the Russian wagons, is not in the wagon works to which I went later. Here there is by comparison an atmosphere of light and a pleasant scent of wood in the air. The feeling of light is accentuated by the colour of the wagons. In the ordinary way they are made of soft wood, such as pine, and painted a dark colour, but the supply of pine has for the moment practically ceased and English oak is being used in its stead, so that the time of Nelson and his ships seems to come round again. How pleased would have been " Cuddie " Collingwood, who carried acorns in his pocket and planted them on his walks that the Navy might not go short. The oaks have been doing good service to their country again, if in slightly less picturesque way. This oak is not painted, and as they leave the Works the wagons look wonderfully bright in their yellow coats, though doubtless they will soon grow as grimy as their elder brethren with hard service.

I promised to say something of the enormous quantity of munition tasks which were added to the normal undertakings of these four railway Works, and now I will try to do so, though it is impossible to do more than touch the fringe. Here I think Eastleigh must have pride of place; Eastleigh which really and truly is a railway town, of which the whole life centres round the works, where the Mayor and his Councillors are railwaymen.

I did not see Eastleigh when the full tide of war-work was surging there, so I must ask the reader to look at it through the eyes of one who did, and for that purpose I use temporarily the present tense.

The shops are now so divided in their allegiance and so transformed from their peace-time aspect as to be almost unrecognizable. Here first are the Locomotive Works and the Paint Shop, where would normally be seen engines still bright and sticky with paint. Now their places have been usurped by gun barrels in various stages of making, while those that are finished are being tested by a Government Inspector. The work on them goes on twenty-four hours a day and seven days a week, and sixty gun barrels are turned out every month. Next is the Brass Shop where railway work and munitions mingle with each other. There are small fittings of all sorts—small parts of locomotives, which represent normal avocations, fittings for torpedo firing gear, tank bushes, and Spitfire floats purely for war. There have been four new machines put up in this shop since war began and the Germans are being hoist with their own petards, since many of the fittings are being turned out by a German machine, the Pittler Lathe.

The Machine Shop is busy with parts for Matilda Tanks and the Boiler Shop with work on motor landing craft and refuelling barges. The landing craft are built at Eastleigh and given bullet-proof coats; they are also fitted with their engines and propellers which are made elsewhere. Here also are Davit Sling Bars for lifting the landing craft and tank bridges which are being made. These thrilling devices are at another stage of development when we get to the Carriage Works. The lower part of the 16-ton tanks are made elsewhere and sent to Eastleigh, where there are added to each of them the turret and the various fittings which take the 30-feet bridge. The tank is kind enough to give an exhibition of its surprising power in a field nearby. It rushes round the field with its bridge folded in half until it reaches the edge of a pit some thirty feet wide. Here it stops while the bridge rises, and slowly unfolds itself. It bridges the pit and at the same time detaches itself from its tank, which then crosses the pit, picks up the bridge again and goes like a triumphant Juggernaut on its way. If there had been many tanks this one would have led the way, laid down its bridge and then waited while the others crossed. Then last of all it would have crossed itself and taken the bridge with it.

The Paint Shop of the Carriage Works is hard at it on aircraft work, turning out the tail ends of gliders, each made to carry 30 to 35 men. The work is begun from scratch, in the shape of spruce logs, and at Eastleigh it began from scratch in another sense ; there were no aircraft workers and the railwaymen started in complete ignorance of aircraft work and quickly mastered it. It would perhaps be more accurate to say the railway women, since, except for the fitting of a skin of plywood over the frame, this work has been done by women, whose numbers rose in the course of one year from 24 to 328 and rose a little later to 400.

That is not a full dress picture, but the most cursory sketch of the munitions work at Eastleigh ; and now back to Ashford for a note on the war work which was done there, apart from that memorable building of wagons for Russia. One important piece of work was the adapting and equipping of mobile workshop units. Each unit consisted of one main workshop, with both fixed machine tools and portable tools in a railway van, a generator in one covered goods wagon, welding apparatus in another, with a third goods wagon to act as a stores van and hold various spare parts. Eighteen such units were turned out at Ashford. There was also the making of 75 ramp wagons for conveying tanks, the repair and conversion of 43 3.7 Howitzers, the repair of rocking bar sights for them, and armour plating for armoured trains. Likewise there was a particularly secret job, involving the making and assembling of a variety of fittings and lifting apparatus, known to its intimates only by its mysterious initials C.D.L. For the Ministry of Aircraft Production there was in particular the making of bomb trolleys, and for the Ministry of Agriculture and Fisheries that of tool-bar-frames for tractors.

Brighton had a considerable amount of contract work for the Government, including steering clutch drums for Infantry Tanks Mark II, Rackam Clutch Steering drums and much detailed work for the equipment of workshop lorries. It also had its great secret and its cryptic initials N.L.E. "I rayther suspect" as Sam Weller would say, that it had something to do with tanks.

It should be pointed out, though it is sufficiently obvious, that Brighton like Ashford was essentially in the front line, since the town was the target of many attacks, chiefly of the tip-and-run order. The Works provided its own Wardens, Decontamination and First Aid Squads, Fire Fighters and so on, who, as well as doing their ordinary work, trained with the greatest energy. They had also their own siren which blew whenever the town had a warning, and that was very often. There were three actual " incidents." In May, 1942, a high explosive bomb did considerable damage, when the whole staff turned to to clear away the debris, so that normal work was going on within 24 hours. In October of that year and in May, 1943, bombs dropped close to the Works and did practically no damage on either occasion; not a single person was killed by bombs and there were very few injuries. Brighton may certainly congratulate itself, but the strain of working under such conditions is not to be measured by the actual damage done.

Lancing, too, did a great deal of miscellaneous work for the Government, beginning in the first months of the war with the conversion of 27 vans and three restaurant cars for Casualty Evacuation Trains, to be used in one of the evacuation schemes that had not to be put into practice. The next year saw amongst other things the making of 100 petrol tanks and another job, which it is pleasant to reflect, was never practically needed, namely the bending of nearly 3,000 old rails for road barriers in case of invasion. There was the manufacture of details of 25-pounder and two-pounder breach mechanisms for the Ministry of Supply, tail plane units for the Air Ministry, various details for motor landing craft for the Admiralty, clutch drums for tanks for the War Office, and so the list might go on for many pages ; it is only possible to pick out odds and ends here and there.

I have tried to set out the respective functions of Eastleigh, Brighton and Ashford in the career of a railway engine. There remains Nine Elms, which has yet another part to play. It keeps the engines running and in repair. The Superintendent is responsible within a certain specified area for providing the right engine to pull any particular train and for producing it coaled and in its right mind at the right time and place.

Constructing landing craft at Eastleigh Works

In the Aircraft construction section at Eastleigh. Many women were employed

One of the goods wagons built at Ashford for Persia. Each part was numbered separately to facilitate erection and replacements

Women workers get sleepers ready for creosoting at Redbridge

Women even took on bridge work

Four different grades of women station workers—guard, porter, cleaner and
ticket collector

Nine Elms is a very important as it is a very impressive place, but a beautiful one it is not. It stands in a corner of Battersea, quite close to the river and just off the main line, whence an engine can pass quickly on to one of the six and twenty lines awaiting it there. Doubtless, as Meg Merrilies said of Derncleugh, " it was a blithe bit ance." Old prints show a pretty little mill and a mill stream and a rustic bridge, part of which is still there though incorporated in a newer structure. There was a farm house just on the other side of the main line and the name of the farmer, Mr. Panton, is still preserved in that of a lane nearby. Somewhere here too asparagus that had come from Holland was first grown in England. These rural amenities are long swept away, and even of the original depot almost all that now remains is a small building still called the clock tower, in which Beattie, one of the great early railway figures, devised his engine. To-day it must be admitted that the place, though not without a certain murky romance, is grim enough. It was perhaps the north-westerly wind that blew when I was there, but a grey canopy seemed to overhang it.

This sombre air has no doubt been enhanced by the war, for if any place had a bad time it was Nine Elms. By a truly merciful circumstance only two men were killed, but there were very many bombs. They have left obvious traces in the gaunt sheds, which come in places to a sudden end. Whole areas that were once under cover and will be again, are now open to the sky, and that means that for the past six years men have had to do out of doors in biting winter winds and sometimes in snow storms what they would once have done within doors. Yet perhaps the most convincing evidence of what Nine Elms suffered is in its immediate surroundings. The visitor gazing over the wall which bounds it on the further side looks on nothing but empty gaping houses. If in all that forlorn view there is a single window to be seen I did not see it. It looks like a little city of the dead. There could have been no more appropriate place to play, as it did during the war, the part of training ground for the Commandos. Here the men would blow up ruins and fight pitched battles in the desert streets, and on one occasion a gentleman perched with a Sten gun in a wrecked house spattered the depot with bullets in a pardonable excess of zeal. Fortunately he did no harm and Nine Elms had had enough bombs to think little of bullets.

WAR WORK IN THE SOUTHERN RAILWAY SHOPS

Aircraft
   Blenheim Conversion Sets.   (Eastleigh.)
   " Horsa "—Tail Plane Units.   (Eastleigh and Lancing.)
   Sets, Sabre Engine Test Beds.   (Eastleigh.)
   M.A. Tail Units.   (Eastleigh.)

Armoured Fighting Vehicles
   Manufacture of parts for Infantry Tanks, Mk. IIA.   (Eastleigh.)
   Scissors Bridge Layers.   (Eastleigh.)
   Details for Matilda Tanks.   (Eastleigh.)
   Steering Clutch Drums for Infantry Tanks, Mk. II.   (Brighton.)
   Tank-locating Gauges.   (Lancing.)
   Rackham Clutch Steering Drums.   (Brighton.)

Guns
   2-pdr. Mk. VII Gun Mountings.   (Eastleigh.)
   2-in. U.P. Mk. II Pillar Boxes.   (Eastleigh and Brighton.)
   Modification of 9.2-in. Howitzer Equipment.   (Eastleigh.)
   Repair and Conversion of 3.7-in. Howitzers.   (Ashford.)
   2-pdr. Mk. X Gun Barrels—machining.   (Eastleigh.)
   Modernisation of 9.2 Rail Truck Mountings.   (Ashford.)
   Drop Stampings for Breech Mechanism.   (Lancing.)

Bridges and Trestles
   Standard Unit Trestles and Column Units for " L " type Trestles (assisting
      L.M.S. Railway).   (Lancing and Ashford.)
   30-ft. Self-launching Bridges.   (Eastleigh.)

Landing Craft and Boats
   Harbour Launches.   (Eastleigh.)
   L.C.S. (M.)   (Eastleigh.)
   L.C.P. (Second Flight Boats.)   (Eastleigh.)
   A.L.C.   (Eastleigh.)
   M.L.C.   (Eastleigh.)
   Fuelling Tenders.   (Eastleigh.)
   Centre Pontoons Assembly.   (Lancing and Eastleigh.)
   Experimental Articulated Pontoon.   (Lancing.)
   Side and Centre Keelsons for A.L. Craft.   (Lancing.)
   Fast Motor Boats.   (Eastleigh.)

WAR WORK IN THE SOUTHERN RAILWAY SHOPS

Railway Vehicles

25-ton Brake Vans. (Ashford.)

Ambulance Trains. (Lancing.)

Tank Ramp Wagons. (Ashford.)

Breakdown Trains for U.S.A. Army by conversion of 40 American Covered Freight Cars. (Ashford.)

Open Goods Wagons for Persia. (Ashford and Lancing.)

Bogie Luggage Vans and Brake Vans converted for use as Casualty Evacuation Trains. (Lancing and Eastleigh.)

Restaurant Cars converted to Staff Mess and Recreation Room Cars for Casualty Evacuation Trains. (Lancing.)

Petrol Tank Wagon Underframes. (Lancing.)

25-ton Goods Brake Vans and Spares. (Lancing.)

50-ton Bogie Warwell Wagons. (Lancing.)

Rail Milk Tanks. (Lancing.)

Cars converted for use on Ambulance Trains. (Eastleigh and Lancing.)

Miscellaneous

8,000-lb. Bomb Trolleys. (Eastleigh.)

Bomb Trolleys, Type E. (Ashford.)

Cradles, Type B to E. (Ashford.)

Cradles, Type A. (Ashford.)

Engine Test Beds and six sets Sabre Mounting Feet. (Eastleigh.)

Tool Bars for Rowcrop Tractors and Ridging Bodies. (Ashford.)

Tank Fittings—Turret Sets and Spares. (Ashford.)

       Turret Sets, assembly. (Ashford.)

       Monoslot Headlamps. (Ashford.)

       Bipods and Accessories. (Ashford.)

Workshop Lorry Bodies—construction. (Eastleigh and Brighton.)

Workshop Lorry Bodies—fitting. (Eastleigh and Brighton.)

Mobile Workshops (conversion of existing vehicles). (Ashford.)

Bent Steel Rails for Road Tank Traps. (Lancing.)

Heat Treatment of Picket Posts. (Lancing.)

Details for Mobile Workshops. (Lancing.)

Mobile Units N.L.E. (Brighton.)

Chapter IX

RAILWAY WOMEN

WHEN I was at Salonica during the last war I used sometimes to watch entranced the stream of all the nations that flowed along the Monastir Road. Most engaging of all, perhaps, were the little family processions within the big procession. In front on the tiny family donkey, his feet nearly touching the ground, rode the head of the household, a gentleman with fierce moustaches, in a blue-braided Eton jacket, a red sash, baggy knickerbockers, and a fez, having the air of a carefree and jovial brigand. Behind, a patient beast of burden with all the household goods on her back, his wife trudged along through the white dust. It seemed hardly a chivalrous or even a fair plan, but perhaps, after all, the Macedonian gentleman knew best. At any rate he had grasped the fact that women make admirable porters.

This war has confirmed his knowledge. By this time we have grown thoroughly used to women porters. At first we felt a twinge of conscience on seeing them whisking our luggage about, and tried to stifle it by saying to ourselves that it was " all knack." Now, though we have never ceased to admire, we are as well accustomed to their feats of strength as we are to their taking our tickets. Perfectly familiar, too, has grown that voice that seems to come from the roof of the station, if not from the heavens above it, telling us all about our trains and platforms and enunciating with a clarity almost too good to be true, the names of all the stations we are going to stop at. We know the kind ladies that sweep the cigarette ends out of our carriage and generally tidy it up before we get in. In short, we have got used to railway women, but what we see and hear of them is but the smallest fraction of what they do, for at the height of their reign the Southern Railway alone has employed ten thousand of them on almost every kind of a job that a man can do, and on many of which nobody before had thought a woman capable.

Of what may be called purely railway jobs they have been booking clerks, goods and parcels clerks, ticket collectors, guards, carriage cleaners, storeswomen and signalwomen. But they have also been employed in big railway works such as those at Ashford and Nine Elms; and at Redbridge, the home of the railway sleeper (to which I shall return later), they largely outnumber the men. Here is a list—I do not suggest for a moment that it is comprehensive—of all the extraneous tasks that they have undertaken: Stablewoman, Oiler and Greaser, Lorry Driver, Blacksmith, Crane Driver, Oxy-Gas Flame Cutter, Electrician, Fitter, Hammer Driver, Oxy-Acetylene Welder, Painter and Policewoman. "Tinker, Tailor, Soldier, Sailor" is nothing to it.

When war began, and as it went on, more and more railway workers were called to the Colours, and more and more women must take their places. In July, 1940, an agreement was made between the Railways and the National Union of Railwaymen as to the employment of women in men's places during the war. Then the flood began to pour in. By 1942 5,000 women had been engaged; by 1944 the number was doubled and amounted to 16 per cent of the whole number working for the Railway. And they have been wonderfully keen, willing and efficient. If they found it hard work at first, as they did, and were sometimes tired and dispirited, they stuck to it and declined to let the job beat them. They came in time to enjoy it, so that many of them will probably be sorry to go back to a wholly different life and to a job easier perhaps but more cramped and lacking something of the old strenuous fellowship.

As has been said before, there are many railway families in which it is as natural for the boys to take to railway work as in other families it is for them to go into the Navy or the Army. This railway blood clearly runs in the veins of the girls as well as the boys, and in this war many women, because they were familiar with the railway tradition, have taken to it like ducks to water. Brighton, for instance, has produced three women passenger guards, of whom one has a father also a guard; the other two, who are sisters, have a father who is an outside porter and a brother who is a parcel porter, and one of them is married to an employee in the Mechanical Engineers' Department. That is keeping it in the family with a vengeance. Those ladies must, as one imagines, have played at railways from their infancy, even as Mrs. Gamp saw Mr. Mould's daughters " playing at berryins down in the shop, and follerin' the order-book to its long home in the iron safe."

To the great majority of recruits, however, the change from their normal lives must have been utter and complete, so that if ever they felt at first " so strange and shy " it was not surprising. How radical the change was may be seen in tracing the vicissitudes of just a very few. A teacher of music became a blacksmith, doubtless a harmonious one, and two of her colleagues in that arduous trade had worked in a greengrocery store and a wineshop respectively. An office worker graduated through mail bags to wielding the mechanical washer on carriages, an employment demanding discretion lest the passengers be drowned. Two nurses and a domestic companion turned into drillers, and the " head kitchen lady " in a catering business was in turn carriage cleaner, porter, and ticket collector. From boarding-house-keeper to announcer, from maid in a girls' school to testing 500 rivets a day, from bookmaker's clerk to welder, from Girton student via professional singing to policewoman—here are transformations of the most sudden. A stewardess on a hospital ship bombed at Dieppe, who had to walk 47 miles to another port to reach home after a five days' voyage in a coaling steamer, may perhaps have found the job of a porter at Brighton, even under tip and run raids, a comparatively placid one. Not that the women wanted placid jobs ; far from it, for when lighter work was given them to begin with, in order to break them in gently, they showed signs of rebellion. The manageress of a baker's shop went to the staff controller and demanded " a real job of work " ; so she was set to drive a 5-ton electric crane, a job that had never been given to a woman before, and she had several imitators, of whom I saw one at Redbridge. A grandmother—a young one, to be sure, for she attained that dignity at 38—looked after horses in the railway's stables at Nine Elms, and there is one lady, Mrs. Brown, who appears to be in a class by herself. What she was before I do not know, but she became the only woman repairer of wagons and does exactly the same work as do the men repairers, such as changing wagon wheels and replacing timber with the use of heavy jacks, and that in all sorts of weather. And so I might go on almost for ever with this record of splendid adaptability and, in vulgar language, guts.

Now and again a round peg would fall at once into a more or less round hole, and a girl who had been in the box office of a theatre stepped naturally into a railway booking office, though perhaps the similarity between the two jobs is more apparent than real. She had to learn the new one, of course, and that brings me to the fact that all these recruits had to be trained, for the most adaptable woman can, no more than could a man, know railway work by the light of nature. Schools were established at Chislehurst, East Croydon, and Victoria where there was given an intensive course of training in general station and office work. There was a model booking office with dummy tickets, dummy notes, and real coins. A booking clerk must learn to be quick, accurate, and handy with these, but that is not all that is demanded of her. She must have a good working knowledge of the geography not only of her own line but of England in general. She must know the difference between Ashford in Kent, and Ashford in Middlesex, and be able to differentiate between the five stations which are all tiresome enough to insist on being called Newport. She must know where the unwary and inexperienced among travellers want to go to even better than they know themselves, and so smooth their paths for them. One by one the pupils would take their places in the model booking office, while the others played at a game of pretending to be passengers, each being duly primed by the instructor with a particularly nasty poser to set the victim for the day's sacrifice. It must have been like that other game of pretending which Oliver Twist played with the Artful Dodger and Charley Bates under the eyes of Fagin. From this school the lady who had already taken her degree at the theatre box office passed in a month, but the usual time was six weeks.

By 1944 there were sixty women passenger guards, and for them there were two schools, one at Victoria and one at Brighton, which seems to have been a peculiarly fruitful ground for recruits, since there, as in other coast towns, the war had brought so many women's work to an abrupt end. In these schools the pupils were taught by an ex-stationmaster the more arid but none the less necessary part of the business, the rules and regulations. Then they passed on to study the real live work by accompanying a guard on his journeys, and finally they took over a train themselves. One young lady, Miss Edwards, had passed all her examinations at nineteen, and was in charge of the train between Charing Cross and Tattenham Corner. In the same way prospective porters began at a school, and then learnt the local conditions at the station at which they were to serve.

Signalwomen were comparatively rare birds, for there were only twenty-four of them when there were 60 guards ; nor is this to be wondered at, for if any reader imagines himself—or herself—set suddenly to railway work he would, as a rule, fight shy of a task so gravely responsible and apparently mysterious. Those who did tackle the job, however, did it very well. I have before me an account by a District Inspector of the teaching of these courageous women, and he has some interesting things to say. For instance, there is, he says, among women less of a " railway sense " than among men. He would doubtless exclude those who came of railway families, and had it in their blood, but generally he found that women had little or no notion of the system of signalling, and so had to begin at the very beginning. I suppose that a passion for trains is much rarer among little girls than little boys, and that they have not so often waited and watched, with an unutterable thrill, for the signalling of their own train. He also thinks that women, when they have learnt something of the business, are a little apt to assume that they have learnt it all, to be, in short, rather superficial and impatient of grounding in principles. Further—and here they will have everyone's sympathy—they were not very good at textbooks and regulations and official language. Having made these criticisms—and psychologists must judge whether they are generally well founded— he has nothing but admiration for their energy and " pliableness " and desire to learn.

It was apparently a good plan for pupils to spend at first some little time in a signal-box, in order to get used to its atmosphere and to see that the work could be done with perfect calm and coolness, and was not so cryptic and alarming as it seemed. Then they had in a waiting-room a simulacrum of a signal box with diagrams, signals made of cardboard, and so on, and were lectured and given notes and oral examinations. They were being trained, as a rule, not for signal- ling in general, but for work in a particular box, so that the dummy box must be laid out on that particular model. The time before they were qualified varied considerably, according to their ages and natural turn for the work, from six to sixteen weeks, and, if one can fancy oneself having to try to learn it, sixteen weeks seems little enough in all conscience. There can be nobody who is not filled with admiration for those who deliberately espoused a task fraught with such responsibility. Brighton, as another feather in its railway cap, has produced the youngest signalwoman, Miss Steel, aged twenty- two, and she was the daughter of a railwayman. She worked at the Old Shoreham Bridge Level Crossing, and also collected tolls and was, in her spare moments, an A.R.P. Warden at Brighton.

So much for what might be called the railway jobs as the passenger thinks of them, but there are also in the background the great Works without which railways could not exist, and here, too, women took the places of men in large numbers. As one striking example, the total number of women that used to be employed at the works at Brighton and Lancing was just eight in all, and during the war-time it rose to 549; 242 at Brighton and 307 at Lancing. Ashford, Eastleigh, Nine Elms, Brighton, Lancing, Exmouth Junction, Redbridge—to all there came women to do hard, heavy, and skilful work in the various mechanical callings, of which I have already given a brief list. They, too, had to be taught, and their teaching depended on the skilled men who had been kept at home. For a man who is hard at work himself to have to teach others is obviously a test of co-operation, to use a now fashionable word, on both sides and one through which both came nobly, generating a fine spirit of team-work and comradeship.

The works at Ashford are chiefly engaged in making and main-taining locomotives and wagons. There were made there in the record time of under ten weeks, a thousand wagons for overseas, each wagon having 1,792 numbered parts, and when that was finished there came another order for 600 12-ton open goods wagons. The work began on December 4th, 1941, and the last wagon was finished on the last day of the year. Those are but two examples of the strenuous labours against time in which women played their part. It was at the beginning of the year, 1941, that women first came to Ashford, and by the end of it there were 200 of them, operating drills and lathes, making underframes for wagons, working as welders, flame cutters, painters, steam-hammer drivers, " and heaven knows what besides." Finally, there were 23 women on the clerical and technical staff and 422 in the workshops. Very often the nature of the work they had to do necessarily revealed its object, as in the case of one special order for North Africa. Those in authority paid the women the compliment of admitting that, contrary to the popular belief and to Thackeray's novels, they could resolutely keep secrets and did not talk.

At Eastleigh by 1944 there were 313 women in the Locomotive Works and 290 in the Carriage Works. Nine Elms had more than 600 women doing all sorts of really heavy work, such as unloading sacks of slate dust (used for the making of Naval grey paint), of which each weighed 140 lbs., and carrying milk cartons, that weighed 28 lbs. each and came in at a rate of 3,000 or 4,000 cases a day. The more one studies such figures the more one realises how right was that Macedonian gentleman on the donkey with whom I began this chapter. And another such arduous task in which women worked at Exmouth Junction was the making of pre-cast concrete units for various uses on the railways, involving 1,000 tons of concrete a year.

As was said before, the only occasion on which these women showed any signs of discontent was when they were not allowed to work as hard as they wanted to, and as hard as the men. They worked long hours, very often in all sorts of weather, and in many places under dangerous conditions from bombing attacks. Their well-being was naturally the subject of much care and thought, and in 1941 a Welfare Supervisor was appointed to look after them. She had, of course, assistants, and in addition, at any place where there were more than a dozen women employed, one of them acted as a liaison officer. The Welfare Supervisor did not actually engage the women, nor did she decide their wages, though she sometimes interviewed applicants for jobs; but there was, altogether apart from that, a very great deal to do. Old buildings must be altered and new ones put up to give proper accommodation and rest rooms. Sick leave and maternity leave, and shopping leave had to be given; and absenteeism, of which there was very little, enquired into. The Welfare Supervisor's was an unending job.

Mention of " shopping leave," which may sound a little curious in the ears of unthinking man, emphasises one final point, on which it would be difficult to lay too much stress, since it is one of the greatest wonders of all. A very large proportion of these women—here the statisticians have, perhaps fortunately, failed me as to the precise number—were married, with households and children to look after. So when they doffed their uniforms or their blue overalls their work was not done, and they had to buckle to once more on domestic duties. Speaking as one who has no cause whatever for any such pride, I know that many men are extremely, and no doubt justly, proud of their feats in making beds and washing up, but even they will, I think, " hand it " to these dauntless ladies of the railways.

As a corollary to this general account of women's work on the railways I will give a particular one of their work as I saw it. The works of Redbridge are on the verge of Southampton. This is a place admirably situated for purposes of transport, since road, rail, and water, the water of the River Test, are all ready to hand. Its task is the fashioning and creosoting of sleepers, but to the outsider its really interesting and almost unique characteristic is that, like Cranford, it is in possession of the Amazons. Roughly speaking, 70 per cent of those employed there are women. And this work is not light work. A sleeper weighs $1\frac{1}{4}$ cwt. and two women lift it and keep on lifting it. A " chair " weighs 46 lbs. and one woman lifts

1,600 chairs in a day. Moreover, if it be not ungallant to say so, these women are not in the first flush of their youth, and some of them have greying hair. The young girls were snapped up by the Services and the work of Redbridge is done by robust matrons. Nearly all of them are married and have families to look after, and incidentally belong themselves, in many cases, to railway families. About a third of them have some relation who works for the railway, so that Redbridge may be said to be on both sides of its pedigree a railway town. They look wonderfully strong and fit, but strength is not all, for they are in charge of machines of precision which need brain and nerve as well. Almost the first thing I saw against the background of tall piles of sleepers was a travelling crane lifting rails from place to place. This was being worked by a woman, the mother of two children, who had lost her husband in the air raids on Southampton.

All machines are equally magical and mysterious, but there was one which had a particularly hypnotic effect on me. It first cut the end off each sleeper—do not ask me how—so as to get it to the exact length, and then planed it, covering me with shavings, and then dropped the sleeper neatly down on to a platform on a lower level where two women were ready to receive it. Next came the really fascinating sight. Each of the two was armed with a " sleeper hook " and as the sleeper fell they simultaneously stuck their hooks into it and pulled it, or rather swung it with one movement to the further end of the platform. Whether one was officially the stroke and the other the bow, or whether it was a case of two minds with but a single thought, I know not ; but no movement could have been more perfectly timed. The heavy sleeper glided across the platform, " as easy as butter," and the spectacle gave that rich satisfaction that comes from watching any skilful athletic performance achieved with the smoothness of long practice, and the minimum of effort. I felt as if I could have watched it for ever ; so when I was led away to the further end of the shop to see something else, I still cast now and then little flickering glances over my shoulder, and the last sight I had was of the two Amazons now high on the top of a still rising layer of sleepers rhythmically plying their hooks.

I saw various other things at Redbridge, struggling to understand, and understanding or thinking I did for a moment of time before the vision was blurred by a new one. I saw, or I believe I did, rails being shaven down—I use quite untechnical language—to the precise width for points and crossings. I saw a machine boring holes in sleepers for bolts, and another that made bolts secure, as it were, with a flick of its wrist. In more technical language, charitably put into my mouth, the women were operating machines for planing and drilling, for gas cutting and precision cutting, for adzing, incising and boring, for sharpening and setting saws.

I saw women whisking chains about as if they were light as air, and a vast cylinder in which the sleepers received their baptism of creosote. But I confess that all these have grown jumbled and dim compared with the picture of those two swinging artists with their sleeper hooks. Twelve o'clock struck and the sturdy figures in blue overalls went off to their dinner and their children, and I went off to my lunch at Southampton, feeling particularly puny and helpless and full of admiration.

Chapter X

MARSHALLING YARDS : FELTHAM AND SALISBURY

THE unthinking traveller may pass Feltham, as he draws near to Staines, without much notice. But Feltham is the Hamm of the south of England. I suppose that before the war and until they became familiar on the wireless, very few of us knew of Hamm or had any very precise notion what a marshalling yard might be. Indeed I gather that even railwaymen themselves did not talk much of marshalling yards, but used some homelier epithet, such as " sorting." However, the B.B.C. has triumphed and marshalling yards they are, now and for ever. As we had heard of Hamm we may be very sure the Germans had heard of Feltham, and indeed, some part of it was built by German prisoners of war during the last war. Having heard of it the enemy tried to do to Feltham as we did to Hamm. They did not achieve so much as we did, but they were not without their successes. They dropped a land-mine there at 3 a.m. one morning, which destroyed about 150 wagons ; but work was begun again by 9 o'clock on the same morning. They hit the " hump " (of which I shall have much more to say presently) and blew the rails over the signal-box. They dropped a 500-pound bomb, which fortunately did not go off, but paralysed all movement in the yard until the Bomb Disposal Squad had picked it up and taken it away. Those are but samples, and when I try to explain, as I am going to do, the work of the yard, the reader must try to picture what it was like in all weathers, at night, in the utter blackness enforced by an alert, and sometimes with bombs falling. I must describe Feltham as I saw it on a fine, peaceful day. In order even to guess what it was like on many days, and especially many nights of the war, the reader must in imagination multiply the difficulties to an indefinite extent.

A marshalling yard may be likened to the Post Office. In place of letters it collects, sorts and distributes wagons to their respective destinations. But Feltham is an exchange as well as a marshalling yard. It receives traffic from the other railway companies through various junctions, sorts the wagons and sends them away by trains to stations on the South Western side of the Southern Railway. Conversely it gathers up trains for other companies and sends them home. It also acts as an inter-sectional exchange for its own stations, but that is by the way; its main and most important dealings are with the other companies. That these dealings are on a large scale a very few figures will show. Feltham has 32 miles of sidings, embracing 73 roads. At the west end are eight " Up Reception Sidings " capable of holding trains of 60 wagons each. At the east end are ten " Down Reception Sidings." Approximately 180 trains, 90 arriving and 90 departing, are dealt with in each 24 hours, but there are special trains as well which are run into both yards as may be necessary. The total number of wagons " turned over " in 24 hours is, roughly speaking, 6,000, 3,000 in and 3,000 out.

And Feltham has no rest. It is as a great engine that never sleeps. The yard is open 24 hours in a day, 7 days in a week, and 52 weeks in a year. In peace time there was a little repose, not much, but a little; the yard could shut down at some period during a week-end, if not the week-end. As soon as war began this was so no longer, and it is to be remembered that much the heavier work falls to be done at night time because the main line is more or less free from passenger traffic. Freight trains (we used to call them " goods trains ") with which the Feltham Yard solely deals, have then more scope. In peace time this is very well, for the yard is bright as day, but with the blackout the strain of the work became incomparably more burdensome. During a " red " warning care had to be taken to avoid, as far as humanly possible, all tell-tale noise such as that of engines whistling or blowing off steam. At best work had to be done by very greatly reduced light, and as soon as the alert sounded even that light must be switched off; darkness was complete. The men unquestionably developed in all yards a mysterious sixth sense by which they could stow accurately away in their memories the order in which wagons were placed and their destinations. On that gift and on hand lamps they had to rely and carry on as best they could unless bombs were actually dropping round them. In the end there was some relaxation and better lighting was allowed at absolutely essential spots, but that was not till the war had been going on for three years.

In peace time again, the work itself was very different. From long experience the yard knew reasonably well what would be coming to it in the next 24 hours. In war time it did not know; it had hardly the faintest notion. There were Government stores trains, tank trains, petrol trains; there were Bailey bridges; there was every conceivable kind of military equipment on its way to docks or depots. In the West of England there were many camps of the Canadian and American Armies, and quantities of their equipment passed through Feltham. It might often pass through twice, going first to Longmoor, a railway station near Aldershot, run entirely by the military, and then coming back on its way to North-Western ports or elsewhere. Of the huge mass of material, familiarly referred to as D-Day stuff, a great deal passed through the yard, and in short, Feltham had to be ready for anything at any time.

Now let me try to describe in a layman's language the ingenious process by which freight trains are split up and wagons are sorted and distributed. The main-spring of the machine is the " hump," that is to say a crest or summit to which a single line of rails gradually rises, with a corresponding fall on the further side. There are two humps, an Up and a Down. Incidentally, for the more exactly minded, the Reception Sidings in the Up Yard are laid out at 1 in 5,000, and there is a gradient of 1 in 40 for 130 feet to the summit of the hump. From the summit to the marshalling sidings there is a fall of 1 in 50 for 170 feet, and then 1 in 156 for 580 feet.

The figures for the Down hump are very slightly different, but that may be allowed to pass. Now for the working of the machine. The reception sidings converge into a single line which climbs the hump. On the other side it leads down hill to a number of marshalling sidings, separate lines or roads, each of which is allocated to a particular destination. These in their turn again converge, so that the train may depart at the further end of the yard, up or down as the case may be. Perhaps a rough simile may be of some help. Let the reader lay his hand palm downwards on the table before him, with his knuckles slightly raised and his fingers spread out. The wagon climbs up the back of his hand till it reaches the knuckles, which are as the summit of the hump, and then runs down one or other of his fingers, whichever may be its allotted road.

Now let us imagine ourselves in the electrically-controlled signal-box, almost opposite the summit of the Up hump, and looking down on the engaging game about to be played there. Some little way off in one of the reception sidings is a long train of wagons. The engine that has brought it so far is not used for humping, and is at liberty to go and have a little rest in the big engine shed. For humping there is another engine, a four cylinder, eight-wheel coupled tank engine, approximately 95 tons dead weight. It takes its place at the rear of the train to be split up, and very carefully and gradually pushes it up the hump. Puff, puff, puff, with much labouring and panting, here comes the long row of wagons at not more than two miles an hour, till it halts at the summit. Now it is the turn of the foreman shunter, with a piece of chalk in one hand and an uncoupling implement in the other. On the front of the first wagon he chalks, let us say, 5, the number of the road which that wagon is to take. On the back of it he chalks 7, to show the road which its immediate successor is to take. After that he chalks the appropriate number on the back of each wagon, so that the signalman knows as each wagon passes him the road of the next one. Thus the shunter goes down the whole line chalking and uncoupling, so that every wagon knows its duty.

Now is the thrilling moment. A wagon freed from restraint is about to run down the slope. The signalman presses a button, click go the points, and here comes the wagon apparently gliding at its own sweet will but in reality obeying the wizard in the signal-box. It seems to be gathering speed, and may run too far or crash into another wagon. This it is not allowed to do, for here is the "brake-chaser" to perform his office. He runs a few yards by the side of the wagon, thrusts his brakestick into its anatomy, and thus prevents it from being indiscreet. Hardly has he retarded one wagon before another is upon him, and he must treat it in the same way.

And so the operation goes on with the smoothness of clockwork. One wagon after another, or sometimes two or three coupled together, since they are for the same destination, follow each other gaily down the slope of the hump to be intercepted and restrained by the "brake-chaser," who must be an athlete and "commando fit." We see them going further away and more and more slowly as the slope decreases, till with perfect manners they bump gently into their predecessors. There will still be a little to be done to them in the way of coupling and so on, in the marshalling sidings, but already there are a number of trains in embryo and the whole process of distributing for 70 wagons or so has taken under ten minutes.

Moreover, when it is all over and the last wagon has gone and the light seems temporarily to have gone out of our lives as we gaze disconsolate at an empty hump, we may look across to the far side of the yard and see the very same thing happening. There are other dear little wagons—for they look quite small in the distance—running along from the Down hump, apparently rejoicing in their freedom, but really doing as they have been told by the magic button. I cannot hope to make the reader understand the lure of this game, for a game it appears ; I can only say that in watching it I felt like all the little boys in all the world who adore engines, and wished that some of them could have been with me in that signal-box.

Now this all happened for my benefit in perfect conditions. To be sure, the wind blew hard, as I am told it nearly always does blow, across that flat expanse where there is nothing to get in its way ; but the day was bright and sunny. Suppose, however, that the wind had blown harder and a very great deal colder ; that there had been snow on the ground, that the sirens had just wailed their warning, and the yard been plunged in inky darkness, the game would not have appeared nearly such a good one ; "game" would have been the least appropriate of words. Yet it was under conditions of this sort that the task had to be undertaken in war-time, over and over and over again. As long as there was no alert, and restricted lighting was allowed, the signalman could see the numbers chalked on the wagons by a powerful electric light in one corner of his box, but in complete black-out that was not possible. Then the signalman could see nothing but the tiny lights of his various buttons, and the shunter had to tell him the numbers by a microphone placed at the summit of the hump. And if those " brake chasers " have a sufficiently vigorous time of it in the best of conditions, what must their work have been like in bitter cold and pitch darkness ? Nobody who is not young and very strong, quite apart from being skilful, could tackle that job, and in fact, young, strong men had to be exempted from military service to do it.

Such is the strenuous and responsible routine of life in a yard, as before to be almost infinitely multiplied in the reader's imagination ; but it has also what my two kind guides called amusing side-lines. Some freight, for instance, is alive. Cattle have labels attached to them, saying when they have last been fed and watered, and if neces-sary, the shunting staff must turn to and water and feed them. Sheep, it seems, can go unfed for thirty hours, but cattle want more attention. Shunters have often had to act as milkmaids, and occasionally even as midwives to delicate cows. Railwaymen seem to be able to take anything and everything in their stride, and I have no doubt they do both to admiration.

Let us add one postscript with the avowed object of making engine-minded little boys, and grown-ups, too, green with envy. The hump is some considerable way from Feltham Station, and those ever thoughtful guides did not want me to have to walk, so I had a brake and an engine all of my own to take me there and fetch me back. Was there ever such bliss, such quintessence of railway romance ? It was the crowning glory of a truly fascinating expedition.

Beyond doubt Feltham was our Southern Hamm, but it must not be allowed to steal all the thunder of all other yards, in which much good work was done, and in particular of Salisbury. The two yards at Salisbury deal with both Southern and Great Western traffic, a task rendered more difficult by a rather complicated lay-out. It had much the same trouble to face as did Feltham in the black-out, and must carry on in utter darkness during plenty of raid warnings. It had in addition to its normal traffic to cope with a great flow of special war traffic, which rose to its height in the months before D-Day. Indeed the work so far exceeded the normal as to call for the appointment of two assistant Station Masters and two additional Inspectors.

There are two yards, the East and the West. The East handles Up West of England trains for Feltham, Southampton, Portsmouth and Brighton; the West Down Main Line trains from Nine Elms, Feltham and Basingstoke, to stations west of Salisbury, and from the south coast to South Wales. In the course of the war a considerable number of sidings were added to the East Yard. In peace time the East Yard could deal with 560 wagons, the West with 250 a day. In war time those figures were increased to 1,000 and 600 respectively, and just before D-Day the East Yard tackled 1,200 a day.

In normal times coal from South Wales passes through Salisbury for the use of the Southern Railway locomotive running depots, and is distributed to all depots from Dover to Devonport. In war time there was, in addition, a transfer of coal from coastal ships to rail for special services, and in this connection Salisbury was an important link between north and south. It also dealt with a number of special trains of cattle to the north and to the south coast, and this traffic was made far more onerous by war-time conditions. There was developed an entirely new traffic in grain in bulk, which would normally have been taken by sea to Southampton Docks. Now it was unloaded from ships at Avonmouth and carried by rail to Messrs. Rank's depot at Southampton. How little does the amateur suspect some of the minor troubles that beset the professional! Despite the best endeavours some of the grain would seep through the bottom of the wagons and produce little crops upon the track to the irritation of the engineers.

Then there were the more directly war-like loads to be carried. There were special trains of all manner of Government stores, petrol, naval and fortress guns, life-boats, anchors (there were sometimes trains of nothing but anchors), barbed wire in whole train loads, and every form of ammunition—shells, bombs, land and sea mines, depth charges and torpedoes. The more nervous inhabitants of Salisbury might have felt their hair standing on end had they realised that one or two trains of aerial bombs passed through their city day after day. Even the calmest of Station Masters must have had his anxious moments, as on one evening when a particularly heavy Government traffic was in process of being handled. There came a red warning, German planes were droning overhead, and a bomb might drop at any instant. None did in fact, an error on the enemy's part, because at that moment this was the state of things. At No. 4 platform there was standing a train of 41 trucks of ammunition ; at No. 2 platform a special train load of bombs and a train load of 473 men ; at No. 1 platform a special ambulance train ; and in the West Yard 35 trucks full of bombs. The red warning lasted some considerable time, and to the Station Master it must have seemed a foretaste of eternity.

This truly formidable traffic was at its heaviest a few months before D-Day, in January, February and March of 1944, when piles of ammunition and stores of all kinds were being accumulated over miles of the surrounding countryside, many of them hidden away under trees in the New Forest. In March, April and May the personnel traffic in turn reached its peak. Neither, of course, did D-Day see the end of it, as witness one particular day soon after it when eighteen special troop trains were received from the Great Western between 7.45 a.m. and 2.0 p.m.

Chapter XI

SPARE TIME JOB
CIVIL DEFENCE

THE whole work of Civil Defence and Air Raid Precautions was done, as far as the Railway was concerned, by men who were also doing their work as railwaymen for long, strenuous hours. The whole immense undertaking of a Railway Company is as vulnerable as it is important. As compared with most other institutions it is difficult to protect adequately, because of its many ramifications and the wide stretch of its activities. Every large railway centre covers a great deal of ground and includes a great number of different buildings. The passenger station with which the traveller is familiar is only one of a whole cluster—offices, warehouses, goods stations, engine sheds and so on, all interdependent, all equally important and equally open to attack and to the ever present danger of fire. Moreover those who have the duty of guarding this complex entity are men who work at different times of day for periods of different length and in times of stress for quite an uncertain number of hours. Therefore the drawing up of a roster of duty for them is clearly a matter of the nicest adjustment and the most detailed and complicated organisation.

The possibility of war threw on the Railway Companies a great number of precautionary duties, but in this chapter I am concerned with one particular point, namely what I may call the spare time jobs of the railwaymen in the task of protecting their railway, as members of the Civil Defence Services, in protecting their country, as members of the Home Guard.

The first of these two tasks had been foreseen, and men had been trained for it before war was actually upon us. Provision had even been made in the early months of the previous war. In the Southern archives is a letter which goes back to the days of the South-Eastern and Chatham Railway. It is dated the 30th October, 1914, from the London District Superintendent's Office at London Bridge, written by Mr. H. E. O. Wheeler, later the Southern's Deputy Traffic Manager, to the Station Master at Charing Cross. It tells him that in case of receiving warning of the approach of hostile aircraft he is to arrange for a responsible man to act as look-out-man on the roof. That look-out-man on Charing Cross roof was the forerunner of a great army of spotters and air raid wardens, of fire, first aid and demolition and decontamination squads.

In the end, out of a staff of 62,000 men, 44,000 had received A.R.P. training, and of those 15,000 had been trained before the war began. On the 29th of June, 1939, a new and to those who saw it an ominous kind of train was standing at number 12 platform on Waterloo Station, a platform then familiar to those taking a train to Southampton to catch an ocean liner, or returning home from a voyage. It was a train of two coaches decorated in bright yellow and bearing in red, black and white letters the message " We've got to be prepared."

This was the Southern A.R.P. Instruction Train. It contained a lecture room and a gas chamber, with sections for stores and living accommodation. There were paraded by it squads of men already trained in the different A.R.P. duties, wearing the clothes appropriate to their respective jobs, in rubber boots and carrying gas masks. It was this train's task to carry instructions to the Southern railwaymen through 68 of their fellows who had been specially trained and had qualified as lecturers. It made peripatetic tours of instruction first to the coasts of Kent and Sussex and then to the West of England. On that day in June already 1,300 railwaymen had received the official Home Office badge for proficiency in decontamination, fire-fighting and demolition work. What most of us probably never thought of was the particular job that might confront the railways in case of a gas attack, namely the decontamination of a whole train ; but the plans had all been made.

Again enormous quantities of A.R.P. stores of all kinds had to be handled by the Railway Stores Department at Lower Road, Waterloo. They need not be all set out here, but there may be quoted one piece of statistics by some ingenious person, one of those calculations which appeal to the taste for the colossal which is in nearly every one of us. By 1942 the A.R.P. stores dealt with at Lower Road would have weighed in all 300 tons and they would have covered a lawn tennis court to the depth of 23 feet. They naturally did not come all at once and if a gas attack had come at once it might have been a close thing. It was at noon on the 2nd of September that the Home Office began to deliver 7,000 respirators. The packing and delivering to the staff who needed them began instantly and went on continuously all night. Lorries and vans as well as staff were borrowed, and by noon on the fateful Sunday, the 3rd, all those 7,000 were in the right hands.

The Railway Company had not forgotten the matter of fire watchers. These had been appointed long before that disastrous December night. Spotters had also come into being and in October of 1940 special four-day courses of training had been arranged for them, at Brighton, Three Bridges and East Croydon. Those who attended these classes had an examination and on passing it a certificate. Old soldiers, if their sight and hearing was good, were chosen for the job and very often fire watchers doubled the part of spotters and could use the fire watchers' post for the purpose. Spotters' warnings were of the greatest value in preventing time from being wasted. A public warning might mean a danger that never materialised and quite unnecessary sheltering, but a spotter's warning meant business ; when, but not until that was heard, it was time to move.

Much had been done, but it was felt that more could be done in the battle against fire, and in June, 1941, Mr. E. M. Turnbull was appointed Fire Officer of the Southern to strengthen the plans for fire fighting over the Company's whole system. He set to work with an office at Waterloo to lay down general principles which the local Chief Wardens should work out in detail. He visited stations and depots everywhere, and called meetings at which every department concerned was represented and he had seven inspectors to help him.

They visited not less than once a month all places at which there were main hydrants or trailer pumps, and all other places in their district once in six months. They gave instruction, arranged for lectures and generally inspired the staff to be " fire-minded." Trailer pumps, hoses and other apparatus were lent to the Company by the Government for the duration of the war ; the fire crews practised constantly and assiduously, sometimes by themselves, sometimes in joint exercises with the local fire service so that the two could, if need be, act as one united team. These exercises were not only frequent—there were roughly some eighty of them a year—but exceedingly realistic. Sham fires were started by means of smoke bombs—a trick which students of Sherlock Holmes will remember was sometimes used by that great man. Such impressive columns of smoke ensued that several times a too well-meaning public summoned the local fire brigade to the rescue.

When after a year the Fire Officer reviewed his labours he could count 131 trailer pumps spread over the whole system at what were deemed the most dangerous points. To serve them were 1,569,000 gallons of water placed in 149 specially erected dams. Besides this there were 71 locomotives and other previously existing tanks to hold nearly 2,700,000 more gallons of water.

All this demanded a great deal of work and kept the fire fighting crews ready for the word " go " for over four years. In a sense it was work that was not wanted since the Germans had in effect thrown up the sponge, as far as the blitz was concerned, in May of 1940, but this is true only in a very superficial sense. Up to almost the last moment there was the incentive for all concerned of believing that they would be very much wanted. Moreover on two occasions they were called on and promptly gave their proofs. One was a fire of unkown origin but not due to the enemy, which broke out in March, 1944, in some huts used by a railway department near Dorking North Station. There was naturally no siren and the fire squad were properly resting, but they dressed in no time and did good work in helping the local N.F.S. to prevent the fire from spreading. The other was in June of the same year when a flying bomb fell on the roof of offices at Victoria and within three minutes a considerable fire was alight. The Station Fire Fighting Squad set to work at once ; the

193

station trailer pump had been damaged by blast, but they brought water from a neighbouring hydrant and in the short space of nine minutes before the N.F.S. arrived they had done much to limit the fire. So they and vicariously at least all their brethren at all the other stations could feel that all their work had been worth while.

HOME GUARD

"There have been many problems and difficulties to be surmounted, the principal one being to decide which was the railway-man's primary duty—to run the railway or to become a soldier. I think it is greatly to the credit of the good humour, common sense and patience of all concerned that this problem has been solved in the right way, which was, of course, that we should continue to run our railway as long as the Nation and the Military Authorities needed it, and then be ready to take up arms to defend it from attack, if the attack ever came." Those words are taken from the General Manager's message to the Southern Railway Home Guard when in December, 1944, the order was given to stand down. They seem to me to state very simply and well the double duty which the railwaymen most willingly undertook.

They had some disadvantages peculiar to themselves. Railwaymen work more or less round the clock but at different times ; they have periodically to work on Sundays and they are liable, especially in war, to be called on for additional hours of duty in emergencies. It was very hard and in some cases impossible to choose times for drills and parades that should suit everybody equally well. It was inevitable that some at least should have to turn out with scarcely a pause after a long day's work. No more could be done than the best possible and it was much to the credit of many tired men that they made the best of it and did turn out.

On the other hand there were advantages, some eminently practical, others more intangible but none the less valuable. Among the former was the fact that there is always a station yard which makes a good place to drill in, and that a station can generally produce at a pinch a room where stores and equipment may be kept. Further there was probably a larger proportion of fairly young men than in most other such bodies because railway work was a reserved occupation.

Among the more indefinite advantages there may be numbered the nature of a railway company which is accustomed to deal with big numbers and to do things on a big scale. It is not likely to be harassed by a problem of organisation. Another great point was that the *esprit-de-corps*, so precious a feature of any such body, which had to grow gradually and did in the end grow splendidly in the Home Guard all over the country, was already there in the case of the Railway Company, full grown from the start. The members might and did come from every branch of the railway service, but they had between them a bond and a common loyalty, the strength of which must strike anyone from outside who is brought into contact with railwaymen. It is the spirit which helps to make a job go, and this one did go. When the Home Guard finally stood down this was the record of the Southern Railway; six Battalions, namely the 28th Kent (1st S.R.), the 25th Sussex (2nd S.R.), the 12th Surrey (3rd S.R.), the 21st Hants (4th S.R.), the 22nd Devon (5th S.R.) and the 36th London (6th S.R.). There were 51 companies and 215 platoons. In addition there were 8 Anti-Aircraft troops (17 light and one heavy) manning 112 light guns and three heavy guns. The total number of men enrolled and trained was 35,510 and the number trained in Anti-Aircraft defence was in all 1,617.

To give at this point that list of ultimate achievement is to go some four years ahead, and we must turn back to the early summer of 1940 when the Home Guard's forerunners, the L.D.V., were formed in answer to the spontaneous and overpowering wish of the Nation. To begin with the Southern L.D.V. were in much the same state as were thousands of others all over the country, a state with which many readers will have been familiar. They had some application forms and not much besides; no uniforms, not even the brassards or armlets which are supposed to do instead, no rifles to drill with. But the men poured in everywhere. At Waterloo, for instance, Mr. Greenfield, who besides being Station Master was Chief Air Raid Warden, took on the job of recruiting and in four days from May the 24th to the 28th, he enrolled 411 men, including the No. 1 recruit, the then Chairman of the Company, the late Mr. Robert Holland Martin, who did his weekly shift of guarding a signal box.

It was on May 22nd that a circular was issued as to enlistment in the L.D.V. and two days later a Headquarters staff was set up at Dorking. A little later Divisional Organisers were appointed for the five traffic divisions of the railway, each with a staff and a number of area organisers. By June 3rd nearly 12,000 men had volunteered and by June 24th just under 17,000, of whom over 8,000 were enrolled. By that time rifles were coming in, though as yet in comparative driblets; 300 for the London area with 200 more promised; 400 for Kent, Surrey and Sussex outside London and 235 provided by external L.D.V. in some country districts. Uniforms were still scarce, 327 all told, but the company provided armlets and ordered steel helmets; a good many men had helmets already. Five miniature ranges had been made and other peoples' ranges were being used. A pleasant commentary on mankind's power of leaving things behind is provided by the fact that about sixty bicycles were obtained from the Lost Property Office for communication purposes. The wheels of training were beginning to go round.

Primarily the men were attested and trained for duty in defence of the railway, but the number of vulnerable points was enormous. Offices, depots, garages, works, signal boxes, flood gates, power houses, bridges, stations and particularly important sections of the permanent way all needed protection. The list prepared showed 402 such points of major, 303 of secondary and 136 of minor importance. A large proportion of the volunteers were engaged at night on their normal railway work, not necessarily at vulnerable points, and even at a vulnerable point a man could not always serve two masters; a signalman could not be in a position to protect his box besides attending to his work. It was therefore impossible at first to provide sufficient guards for all points and owing to the scarcity of rifles armed guards were for the moment out of the question. Yet by the end of June a good deal had been done. 121 points on the railway were guarded by the Army, but railway volunteers provided armed patrols at 268 points and unarmed patrols at 220.

There was to begin with a certain difficulty of organisation and discipline. Theoretically every railway section or platoon formed part of the general L.D.V. organisation of its town or district; but practically the question of points on the railway to be guarded could only be decided by the Divisional Organisers of the railway, and they had no military status. There were possible means of giving them that status but the difficulty was resolved in a much more satisfactory way when the authorities decided to treat the Railway Units as separate entities under their own Commanders. Early in July there were various meetings at the War Office and the scheme for the six battalions was approved. These were formed on geographical lines, the first battalion having its headquarters at Orpington, the second at Haywards Heath, the third at Woking, the fourth at Southampton, the fifth at Exeter and the sixth at Waterloo. Subsequently they became battalions of the six distinguished regiments already enumerated and wore their badges. It should be added that much of the original organisation was done by Mr. F. J. Wymer, who was made C.B.E. in recognition of his work, and when he resigned the command of the Southern Group he was succeeded by Mr. S. H. Isaac.

Some of these initial difficulties were peculiar to the railway units, but in general their growing pains were those of the other Home Guard units and so need no especial description. They were gradually overcome as others overcame them, and in course of time the S.R. H.G. not only protected all the Company's property, a duty in which they were specialists, but also attained a sound general knowledge of soldiering.

The Home Guard had scarcely been formed when it blossomed out into an illustrated paper of its own. This paper, originally called " Southern on Guard " and later " Southern Home Guard," appeared every two months, devoted entirely to the activities of the various battalions, social as well as military, their competitions and leading personalities. Here was to be found the roll of honour of members who had been commended for some meritorious action, from putting out incendiary bombs to vigilance in detecting thefts from automatic machines. Individual members wrote short articles, some serious and some light-hearted. One pleasant and recurring feature was founded on the detective, Dr. Morelle, who was familiar to all who listened in to " Monday Night at Eight " on the wireless. There were invasion exercises ; the " Outlanders " had invaded the country and Sergeant Worelle was in command of a party guarding a strong point. To him would appear some apparently guileless homeguardsman from another battalion bringing orders to retire. The Sergeant, having his suspicions, engaged him in conversation and soon convicted him, the clue that had enabled him to do so being given on another page. For example the spy had incautiously stated that he was a fireman on the railway and had fired a Lord Nelson locomotive between Charing Cross and Hastings. That was a sad blunder; Lord Nelsons do not run on that route because of the narrowness of one of the tunnels. The spy had been too clever by half.

Another product of enthusiasm was the formation in 1941 of a Band, possessing the fine sonorous title of the " Corps of Drums," the first Home Guard Band of any of the Main Line Railway Companies. After marching at a parade to the strains of the band of the Coldstream Guards there arose among the men an ambition to cheer up their own route marches by their own music. Subscriptions of a penny a week were invited towards buying the instruments and the Company advanced the money against the promises received and subscribed themselves. There were fortnightly practices, at first under a Sergeant of the Coldstream and presently the Band were prepared to go anywhere to play " the spirit-stirring drums, the ear-piercing fife " at Home Guard parades.

The eighteen Anti-Aircraft troops (seventeen light and one heavy) of the S.R. H.G. have already been mentioned but must have a special word. They belong to a later period of the war, which gave to the Home Guard not only the chance of releasing regular soldiers for other duties in the field, but that for which they had dearly longed, of themselves getting in a blow at the enemy. The number of " Southern on Guard " for April and May, 1943, bears right across the front page a flaming headline " S.R. H.G. Ack-Ack ", and beneath is the triumphant announcement: " We have entered the Ack-Ack family and produced a new offspring—B Troop, to be precise—of a H.G. Anti-Aircraft Battery." This forerunner of a fine family was " B " (S.R.) Troop 71st Hants and Isle of Wight Heavy A.A. Battery, and of all the best possible days of the year, on St. George's Day, in 1943, they went into action for the first time. It was at nine o'clock on a wet, dark night that they received the alarm " Take Post " and as soon as the enemy was within range they opened fire. The enemy soon made off, leaving the battery with a heart-warming sensation of having justified their existence.

One of the great features of the H.G. S.R. was the Camp at Gomshall in Surrey, quite close to the Station, which was at different times inspected by two Generals successively holding the South Eastern Army Command, and inspired a Leading Parcel Porter in one number of " Southern On Guard " to drop into poetry as a friend. Preceded in the earlier days by a school of training in Osterley Park, it was originally opened in the time of the blitz to help Southern home guardsmen to get away and do their training at week-ends in relatively peaceful surroundings. Gradually it blossomed into a whole time institution. It had a standing staff of a Camp Commandant, a R.S.M., a Sergeant-Cook, and another Sergeant who combined the offices of range warden and barman. It afforded a varied course of instruction, given both by Officers of the Battalion and Officers and N.C.O's from a Canadian Training School. There was a regular weekly course from Monday to Friday for leaders, potential leaders and weapon-training instructors, and a week-end specialised course for Battalions. The Railway released each week twenty-four men to attend the school, without loss of pay, and with their travelling expenses. They lived, as was appropriate, in converted coaches and had besides plenty of games from billiards to dominoes, a canteen, a mess room, and a lecture room, a full bore range out of doors and a miniature range indoors. Here is a syllabus of the week's training :—

> Monday—Sten M.C. firing positions, anti-tank rifle fire control.
>
> Tuesday—Grenades (all types) theoretical and live practice on bombing range.
>
> Wednesday—Platoon in attack. Camouflage. Intelligence.
>
> Thursday—Battle drill. Battle craft.
>
> Friday—Range firing.

This mid-week Camp was naturally small by comparison with that at the week-end when about a hundred railwaymen would assemble weekly. It was a cheerful, assiduous and eminently democratic assembly in which all ranks in the railway world were merged and forgotten. It began at 4 o'clock on a Saturday afternoon with potato peeling, a task which, so it is basely rumoured, some people avoided by finding themselves too busy to catch an early train. After that came tea and then a series of three lectures, each of half to three quarters of an hour, given by N.C.O's, most of them from the six Battalions but some from outside. Then came a dinner-cum-supper meal and after that freedom till lights out.

Having thus been broken in gently the Camp fell early to strenuous work on the Sunday morning. The men were up at 6.30, had a cup of tea and then came P.T. Breakfast was at 7.30. After that came the throwing of dummy grenades for half an hour as an introduction to live ones. After that again sten gun practice or, if the weather was wet, a lecture. At 11.30 there was a break for coffee and there was certainly no lack of good food, for one of my informants, though a little vague as to precise details, is prepared to swear that he had seven meals in twenty-four hours. This particular meal being over, there came practice on the full bore range, for which the sandy cliffs, that are a familiar sight near Gomshall Station, made a convenient background. That filled up the time till another meal. Dinner at 1 o'clock, and nobody can say that the morning had not kept everybody's talent well employed. After dinner from 2 to 3.30 there was a general process of cleaning up and at 4.30 the day was over and the train steamed away.

Such very briefly was the week-end routine. The Camp was not only a place of hard and conscientious work but also a holiday camp in the sense that the best holiday is a change of work. The holiday, for the inside of a week, had the advantage of being a free one and it helped to make new friendships between railwaymen from different parts of the country who had never met before but were the more ready to make friends from their common bond of service. That was a bond which had stood the Southern Home Guard in good stead in 1940 when they set out on an adventure of which no man could foretell the end. It had become stronger and more enduring than ever when in 1944, after five strenuous years, they stood down, conscious of a duty well done.

SOME OTHER ACTIVITIES

Civil Defence and the Home Guard formed the railwayman's most obvious and most urgent activities in the little leisure that he had, but there was a number of others which he managed to crowd into his time to help the sum total of the war effort. For instance he collected and contributed a great deal of money to good causes, in particular the penny a week Red Cross Fund, and his own P.O.W. Fund for the men of the Southern who were taken prisoner. As soon as the Lord Mayor had made his appeal to help the sick and wounded, steps were taken in March, 1940, to organise a worthy response. As a result by giving a penny a week from their wages the Southern Railway staff had contributed in the end £55,769. Nor was that all for by means of fetes and other such entertainments they added a further £5,250. It is impossible even to begin to enumerate these efforts, but I may say a word about just one, to stand for many. In 1941 a shunter and a porter had a sing-song in the Priory Hotel at Dover and passed the hat round afterwards. That modest start grew into a monthly concert, something in the nature of a glorified village concert with songs and accordion solos, the music provided in general by railway talent, with occasional help from the miners of Aylsham. There were draws for prizes given by various kind people and other such familiar features, and though the room was quite a small one the money for the Red Cross and the P.O.W. Fund steadily rolled in. Shells, bombs and " doodle-bugs " were occasional accompaniments but the concerts went on undaunted. Christmas, 1944, saw the grand culmination when a big hall was taken to hold 400 or 500 people, and when the concerts finally ended the once apparently impossible target of £1,000 had been reached.

Then there was the giving of aeroplanes, and here the Southern had the honour of being the first British Railway Company to give a Spitfire. It was in August of 1940, just when we at home were beginning fully to realise the value of Spitfires in the Battle of Britain, that the Southern staff was asked to buy a fighting aircraft. No sooner said than done ; the Southern Spitfire was at once forthcoming and was christened " Invicta " after the first locomotive on the Canterbury and Whitstable line, the earliest forerunner of the Southern Railway.

The appetite for aeroplanes came in the buying. Why not one for the Fleet Air Arm as well as the R.A.F. ? In 1942, a Fulmar, D.R.659, made its appearance. The givers were kept informed of the deeds of their planes. They were told how the "Invicta," in escorting bombers, had a lively battle with some Focke Wulfes and though not unscathed continued to do good service. D.R.659 had an exciting time in protecting a famous Malta Convoy, and came through as did the convoy. And to complete this generous story, each of the various departments of the Railway adopted one of the Company's ships that figured so bravely at Dunkirk and on D-Day, and subscribed every week towards comforts for the crews.

Railwaymen had a special fund for their own brethren who were prisoners. By its means each prisoner received every month 500 cigarettes and 1 lb. of tobacco, and in addition a more gorgeous parcel every quarter. He also got a personal letter telling him as far as possible the sort of thing he would like to know from home. Books were sent too, mostly fiction but also educational for those who wanted them; likewise indoor games and packs of cards. Those who were lucky enough to be repatriated were given cheques to represent the parcels that they had not been able to receive. Ladies who were members of the staff, and their friends, knitted assiduously, and the garments they made were regular features of the parcels. Here again money was raised for the good cause in all sorts of ingenious ways, such as an entertainment at the Eastleigh Works when two of the latest locomotives were displayed and explained, and members of the public could pay for the joy of blowing the whistle.

The story is far from ending with that triumphant blast, for the War Savings movement had a generous response. In all the "Salute the Soldier," "Wings for Victory," and other such weeks, the names of which have now grown a little dim, the Southern staff regularly set up their targets and as regularly knocked them down with something to spare. At one particular station the target sum was multiplied by eight. By 1944 there were already over 600 savings groups in existence. A year before that the Southern Railway had earned a certificate of honour for having raised in "Wings for Victory" alone £800,000. Apart from the contributions of the staff, Stations lent themselves to the helping forward of such campaigns; they provided good selling centres for their passengers, who were gently persuaded by such pleasant little jokes as the issue at Tunbridge Wells of souvenir tickets, white and green, first and third class, for one soldier to Berlin " on the Invasion Special."

Lastly I come to a more strictly peaceful avocation, though an invaluable one in war time, that of allotments. There had always been many line-side plots and it is on record that one worthy old gentleman, as he may by this time be respectfully termed, has had an allotment by Ore station since 1888. Now, though many of those who cultivated their little gardens were away on service, the number of allotments increased steadily until by 1943 there were 600 acres of them, with over 13,000 plots. Railwaymen have always been keen gardeners and the Company having ground to spare for the purpose, let it to the staff on almost nominal terms. How keen they were may be gathered from the fact that in an allotment show in the Southampton area there were 339 entries, of which 140 came from railwaymen. "All line" competitions between teams of five men each showing twelve vegetables were very popular, and in one of them Basingstoke alone provided three teams. There were shows in many places, and it was not merely the growers of the vegetables who profited but many Railway and Forces charities as well. Incidentally the travellers at London Bridge Station were asked to leave any surplus from their gardens there for the benefit of Guy's Hospital, and the invitation was most liberally accepted. Some war-time impressions pass quickly with peace and the motto "Dig for Victory" has now an almost archaic sound, but it was a very important one in its day, and the railwaymen acquitted themselves like men and good diggers.

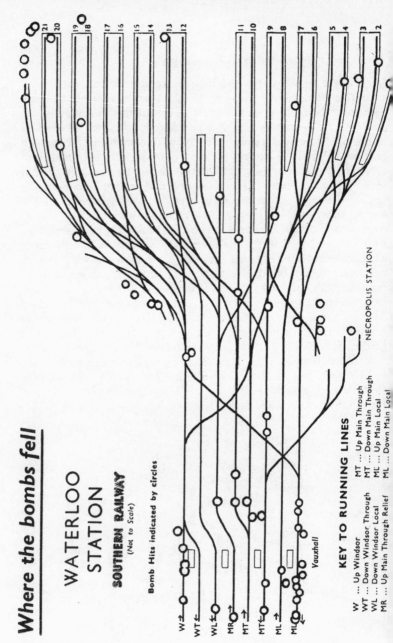

Where the bombs fell

WATERLOO STATION

SOUTHERN RAILWAY
(Not to Scale)

Bomb Hits indicated by circles

W ⇄ ... Up Windsor
WT ⇄ ... Down Windsor Through
WL ⇄ ... Down Windsor Local
MR → ... Up Main Through Relief
MT → ... Up Main Through
MT ⇄ ... Down Main Through
ML → ... Up Main Local
ML ⇄ ... Down Main Local

Vauxhall

NECROPOLIS STATION

KEY TO RUNNING LINES

W ... Up Windsor
WT ... Down Windsor Through
WL ... Down Windsor Local
MR ... Up Main Through Relief

MT ... Up Main Through
MT ... Down Main Through
ML ... Up Main Local
ML ... Down Main Local

AIR RAID WARNINGS (RED) IN EACH OF THE 29 SOUTHERN RAILWAY WARNING DISTRICTS, 1939/1945

WARNING DISTRICT	1939	1940	1941	1942	1943	1944	1945	TOTAL
1. Canterbury ...	2	530	861	402	356	132	20	2,303
2. Folkestone ...	1	530	864	606	475	162	5	2,643
3. Maidstone ...	1	430	403	83	154	176	30	1,277
4. Tunbridge Wells	1	334	238	37	141	140	2	893
5. Hastings ...	1	334	256	311	358	152	—	1,412
London—								
6. (East) ...	2	384	151	33	114	463	45	1,192
7. (Croydon) ...	2	392	115	24	111	511	16	1,171
8. (Central) ...	1	414	139	26	95	508	23	1,206
9. (South) ...	2	354	87	18	87	332	12	892
10. (West) ...	1	261	72	13	62	272	8	689
11. Horsham ...	1	234	87	34	113	217	1	687
12. Brighton ...	1	306	180	171	189	163	—	1,010
13. Reading ...	—	52	71	18	40	60	1	242
14. Aldershot ...	1	151	84	37	70	160	1	504
15. Guildford ...	1	151	84	29	72	177	—	514
16. Worthing ...	1	347	369	190	175	131	—	1,213
17. Basingstoke ...	—	75	83	41	51	59	—	309
18. Portsmouth-Southampton	—	347	427	379	228	136	—	1,517
19. Andover ...	—	75	79	24	29	33	—	240
20. Salisbury ...	—	63	108	81	58	30	—	340
21. Bournemouth	—	168	220	323	162	39	—	912
22. Yeovil ...	—	78	118	91	54	13	—	354
23. Weymouth ...	—	126	179	229	113	22	—	669
24. Taunton ...	—	—	33	18	8	3	—	62
25. Exeter ...	—	42	145	135	98	18	—	438
26. Barnstaple ...	—	5	98	13	9	3	—	128
27. Okehampton	—	231	113	15	19	6	—	384
28. Bodmin ...	—	97	103	15	17	5	—	237
29. Plymouth ...	—	231	261	75	29	21	—	617

ENGINES, CARRIAGES AND WAGONS

From outbreak of war to 14th July, 1945

Locomotives on hand at outbreak of war 1,819

New locomotives built for Southern Railway use ... 65

> 1 'Q' Class
> 40 'Q1' Class
> 20 'Merchant Navy' Class
> 4 'West Country' Class

Locomotives destroyed by enemy action 1

Locomotives damaged by enemy action... 189

Locomotives built by Southern Railway for other Companies 130

Carriages destroyed by enemy action—steam 49 ⎫
                                     electric 93 ⎬ ... 153
Non-passenger-carrying coaches   „   11 ⎭

Carriages damaged by enemy action—steam 1,806 ⎫
                                   electric 1,784 ⎬ ... 4,040
Non-passenger-carrying coaches   „   450 ⎭

Mobile Railway Workshops equipped ... 23 Units (90 vehicles)

Hospital Coaches equipped for forces 138

Casualty Evacuation Coaches equipped 68

Wagons built for Government use overseas 1,600

Wagons built for Government Departments 285

Wagons built in S.R. Shops for work in this country :—

> For S.R. ... ... 7,300 ⎫
> „ L.M.S. ... 1,755 ⎬ 11,935
> „ L.N.E. ... 2,230 ⎪
> „ G.W.R. ... 650 ⎭

Wagons destroyed by enemy action ... 145 ⎫ ... 169
Service vehicles ... ... 24 ⎭

Wagons damaged by enemy action ... 1,249 ⎫ ... 1,355
Service vehicles ... ... 106 ⎭

Privately owned wagons destroyed by enemy action on S.R. 69

Privately owned wagons damaged by enemy action on S.R. 800

NAVAL AND MERCHANT VESSELS REPAIRED AT SOUTHERN RAILWAY MARINE WORKSHOPS

SOUTHAMPTON :

H.M. Ships	184
Merchant Ships	723
Water Ambulances	50
	957

Analysis of Repairs, etc.

Major refits to H.M. Ships, Passenger and Load Line Surveys	66
Major damage repairs to H.M. Ships and Merchant Ships	55
Periodic overhauls and boiler cleaning	128
Voyage repairs to Merchant Ships and maintenance of Water Ambulances	697
Original fitting out of H.M. Magnetic Minesweepers	11

NEWHAVEN :

H.M. Ships	603
Merchant Ships	140
Hospital Carriers	10
R.A.F. High Speed Launches	21
	774

Analysis of Repairs, etc.

Major refits to H.M. Ships, Passenger and Load Line Surveys to Merchant Ships	74
Major damage repairs to H.M. Ships and Merchant Ships	90
Periodic overhauls and boiler cleaning	460
Voyage repairs to Merchant Vessels and maintenance of Hospital Carriers	150

H.M. Vessels comprised Patrol Boats, Motor Launches, Motor Minesweepers, Motor Torpedo Boats, Motor Gun-boats, etc., and all types of Landing Craft. Repairs to other small craft were also carried out.

DOVER :

The Dover Marine Workshops, with the S.R. staff, were taken over and controlled by the Admiralty from July 1st, 1940, to January 31st, 1945, and can claim a large share of the work of keeping the Dover Patrol and its auxiliaries at sea. In addition, service overhauls, boiler cleaning and running repairs were carried out to the various transports and auxiliary vessels positioned at Dover.

COAL FOR LOCOMOTIVES AND POWER HOUSES

How the S.R. built up its stocks for D-Day

Average weekly use pre-war was 20,000 *tons for locomotive purpose and* 2,000 *tons for power houses*

	TONS
Stock at outbreak of war	109,172
„ by May, 1940	118,142
„ „ August, 1940	133,143
„ „ August, 1944	141,432
Stock at the end of the war in Europe (equivalent to little more than two weeks' supply)	48,086

Coal by Sea

Normally, an average annual supply of 37,500 tons of coal for locomotives is shipped from South Wales and other coaling ports to the Southern Railway ports of Fremington (20,000 tons), Cowes (6,500 tons) and Portsmouth (11,000 tons). During the war, owing to munition-congested rails, enemy action, shortage of wagons, etc., this total was increased to 301,931 tons. The additional tonnage was handled as follows :—

Port of entry.	1941.	1942.	1943.	1944.	1945.	Total.
	Tons.	Tons.	Tons.	Tons.	Tons.	Tons.
Southampton...	39,925	25,476	58,623	13,159	806	137,989
Newhaven ...	—	—	6,278	2,304	—	8,582
Fremington ...	—	16,158	22,294	14,758	—	53,210
Highbridge ...	3,113	25,747	24,001	11,789	—	64,650
Total ...	43,038	67,381	111,196	42,010	806	264,431

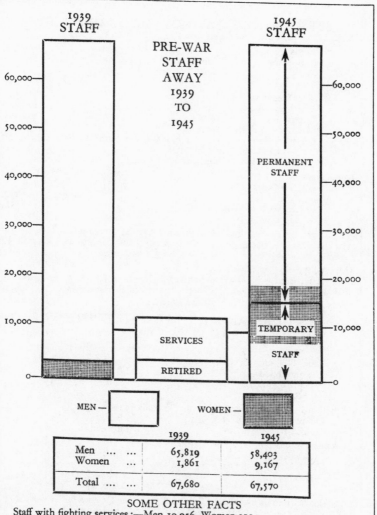

	1939	1945
Men	65,819	58,403
Women ...	1,861	9,167
Total	67,680	67,570

SOME OTHER FACTS

Staff with fighting services :—Men 10,956, Women 212.
Staff killed on active service :—Men 387.
Staff killed by enemy action on railway duty :—Men 170.
Staff injured by enemy action on railway duty :—Men 687, Women 59.
Staff retained beyond normal retiring age :—Men 3,926, Women 11.

SUBSCRIPTIONS, SAVINGS, ALLOTMENTS, ETC.

Subscriptions   £

   For purchase of a " Spitfire " aircraft   5,000

      ,,   ,,   ,,   " Fulmar " aircraft 5,000

Savings

   " War Weapons " Week 607,500

   " Warship " Week 618,420

   " Wings for Victory " Week 814,888

   " Salute the Soldier " Week 852,000

   3 per cent. Defence Bonds purchased by the Southern Rail-

     way Co. on behalf of Staff 35,780

   There are over 600 Savings Groups throughout the S.R. System.

Red Cross

   " Penny-a-Week " Fund 56,655

   Special Shows 5,250

   Red Cross Coach Tour... 655

Dig for Victory

   Southern Railway line-side allotments, 13,793, covering 602 acres.

   During the war over 30 staff Allotment Associations were formed at various places on the system, each covering a wide area.

Ship Adoption

   Each principal railway department adopted a S.R. ship chartered to M.W.T., and supplied comforts, periodicals, etc., to the crews.

HONOURS AND AWARDS TO SOUTHERN RAILWAY STAFF

a. National Honours for Railway work :—

Knighthood	1	M.B.E.	...	15
C.B.E. ...	1	B.E.M.	...	55
O.B.E. ...	3			

b. National Awards for gallantry on the Railway :—

George Medal	7	M.B.E.	...	1
B.E.M. ...	25	Commendation		42

c. Awards to staff on chartered steamers :—

D.S.C. ...	7	M.B.E.	...	1
D.S.M. ...	2	B.E.M.	...	6
O.B.E. ...	4	Mentioned in		
		Despatches		10

d. National Honours awarded to S.R. Staff on Home Defence duties, including Civil Defence and Home Guard (apart from awards granted under *b* above) :—

G.M.	...	2	B.E.M. ...	4
C.B.E.	...	1	Commendation	1
M.B.E.	...	6		

INDEX

INDEX

INDEX

INDEX

INDEX